Windows Server 2008 Administrator

Lab Manual

WILEY

EXECUTIVE EDITOR	John Kane
EDITORIAL PROGRAM ASSISTANT	Jennifer Lartz
DIRECTOR OF MARKETING AND SALES	Mitchell Beaton
PRODUCTION MANAGER	Micheline Frederick
PRODUCTION EDITOR	Kerry Weinstein
DEVELOPMENT AND PRODUCTION	Custom Editorial Productions, Inc.

To order books or for customer service, please call 1-800-CALL WILEY (225-5945).

ISBN 978-0-470-22510-3

Printed in the United States of America

10 9 8 7 6 5 4 3 2 1

BRIEF CONTENTS

CONTENTS

Lab 6. Working with Disks   83

Lab 7. Using High-Availability Features   99

LAB 1
DEPLOYING WINDOWS SERVER 2008

This lab contains the following exercises and activities:

BEFORE YOU BEGIN

The classroom network consists of Windows Server 2008 student servers that are all connected to a local area network. There is also a classroom server, named ServerDC, that is connected to the same classroom network. ServerDC is also running Windows Server 2008 and is the domain controller for a domain named contoso.com. Throughout the labs in this manual, you will be working with the same student server on which you will install, configure, maintain, and troubleshoot application roles, features, and services.

Your instructor should have supplied you with the information needed to fill in the following table:

Student computer name (Server##)	
Student account name (Student##)	

Working with Lab Worksheets

Each lab in this manual requires that you answer questions, shoot screen shots, or perform other activities that you are to document in a worksheet named for the lab, such as lab01_worksheet. Your instructor will supply you with the worksheet files by copying them to the Students\Worksheets share on ServerDC. As you perform the exercises in each lab, open the appropriate worksheet file using WordPad, fill in the required information, and save the file to your computer's Student##\Documents folder. This folder is automatically redirected to the ServerDC computer. Your instructor will examine these worksheet files to assess your performance.

The procedure for opening and saving a worksheet file is as follows:

1. Click Start, and then click Run. The Run dialog box appears.

2. In the Open text box, key **\\ServerDC\Students\Worksheets\lab##_worksheet** (where lab## contains the number of the lab you're completing), and click OK.

3. The worksheet document opens in Wordpad.

4. Complete all of the exercises in the worksheet.

5. In WordPad, choose Save As from the File menu. The Save As dialog box appears.

6. In the File Name text box, key **lab##_worksheet_*yourname*** (where lab## contains the number of the lab you're completing and *yourname* is your last name), and click Save.

SCENARIO

You are a newly hired administrator for Contoso, Ltd., working on a test deployment of the application server technologies included with Windows Server 2008. In this lab, you examine some of the tools you can use to deploy Windows Server 2008 to computers on the network.

After completing this lab, you will be able to:

■ Install the Windows Deployment Services role

■ Use the Windows Deployment Services console

■ Install the Windows Automated Installation Kit

■ Use the Windows System Image Manager

Estimated lab time: 130 minutes

Exercise 1.1	Performing Initial Configuration Tasks
Overview	You are currently setting up a new computer that was delivered with Windows Server 2008 already installed in its default configuration. Your first task is to configure the computer with appropriate settings for the test lab network.
Completion time	10 minutes

1. Turn on your computer. When the logon screen appears, log on using the local Administrator account and the password *P@ssw0rd*. The Initial Configuration Tasks window appears, as shown in Figure 1-1.

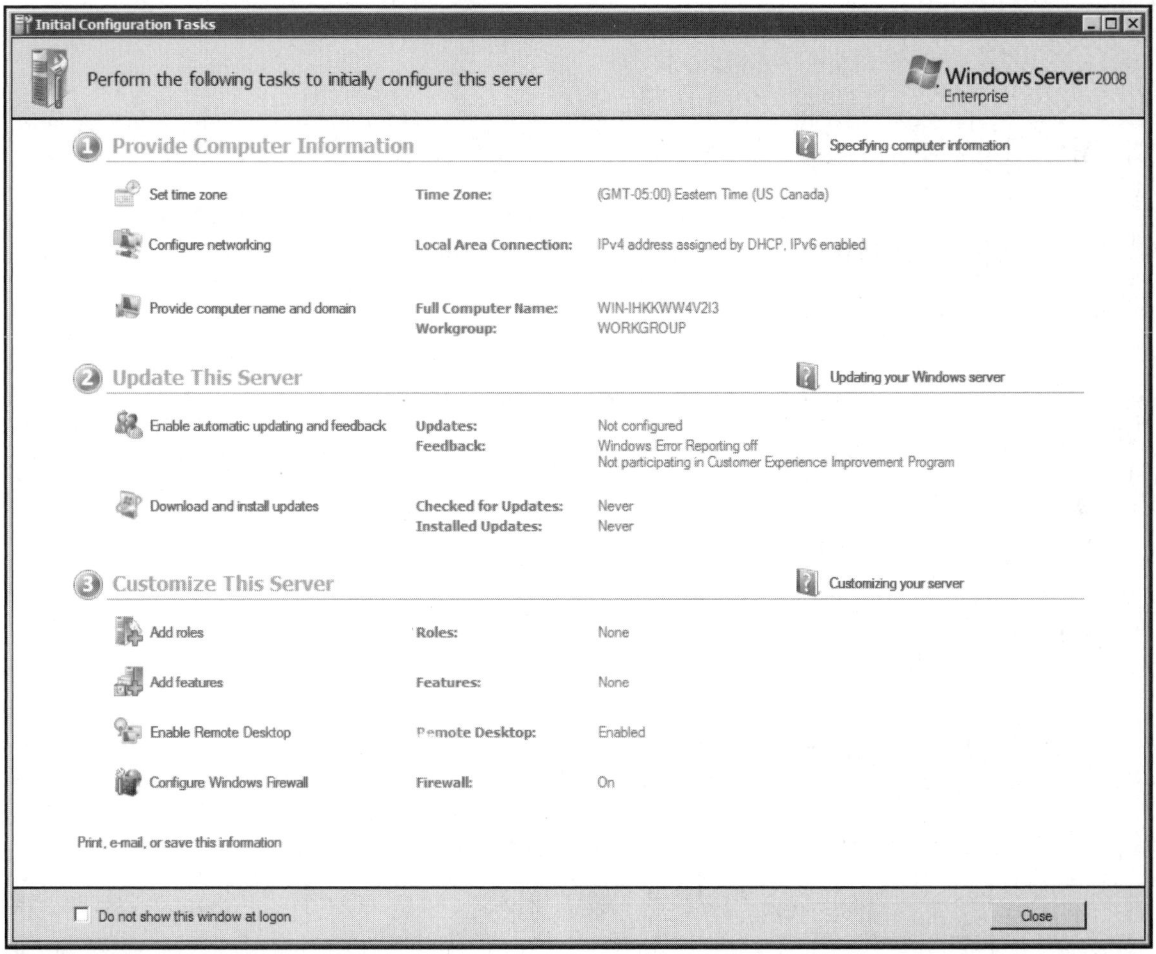

Figure 1-1
Initial Configuration Tasks window

2.   Click Set time zone. The Date and Time dialog box appears.

3.   Make sure that the date, time, and time zone shown in the dialog box are correct for your location. If they are not, click Change date and time or Change time zone and correct them. Then click OK.

4.   Click Provide computer name and domain. The System Properties dialog box appears with the Computer Name tab selected.

5.   Click Change. The Computer Name/Domain Changes dialog box appears.

6.   In the Computer name text box, key **Server##**, where ## is the number for your computer supplied by your instructor.

7.   Select the Domain option. In the text box provided, key **contoso.com**, and click OK. A Windows Security dialog box appears.

8.   In the User Name text box, key **Administrator**. In the Password text box, key **P@ssw0rd**, and click OK. A message box appears after a brief delay, welcoming you to the contoso.com domain.

Question 1	Which computer is hosting the Administrator account that you are specifying in this authentication?

9.   Click OK. A message box appears, prompting you to restart your computer.

10.   Click OK, and then click Close to close the System Properties dialog box. Another message box appears, informing you again that you must restart the computer.

11.   Click Restart Now. The computer restarts.

12.   Log on to the domain with your Student## account, where ## is the number assigned by your instructor, using the password *P@ssw0rd*.

13.   Press Ctrl+Prt Scr to take a screen shot of the Initial Configuration Tasks window, and then press Ctrl+V to paste the resulting image on the page provided in the lab01_worksheet file.

14.   Leave the computer logged on for the next exercise.

Exercise 1.2	Using Server Manager
Overview	In the future, you will need to configure your server to perform certain tasks by using tools and services that Windows Server 2008 does not install by default. Your task in this exercise is to use the Server Manager console to configure the server and install these tools and services.
Completion time	10 minutes

1. Click Start, point to Administrative Tools, and click Server Manager. Click Continue in the User Account Control message box. The Server Manager console appears, as shown in Figure 1-2.

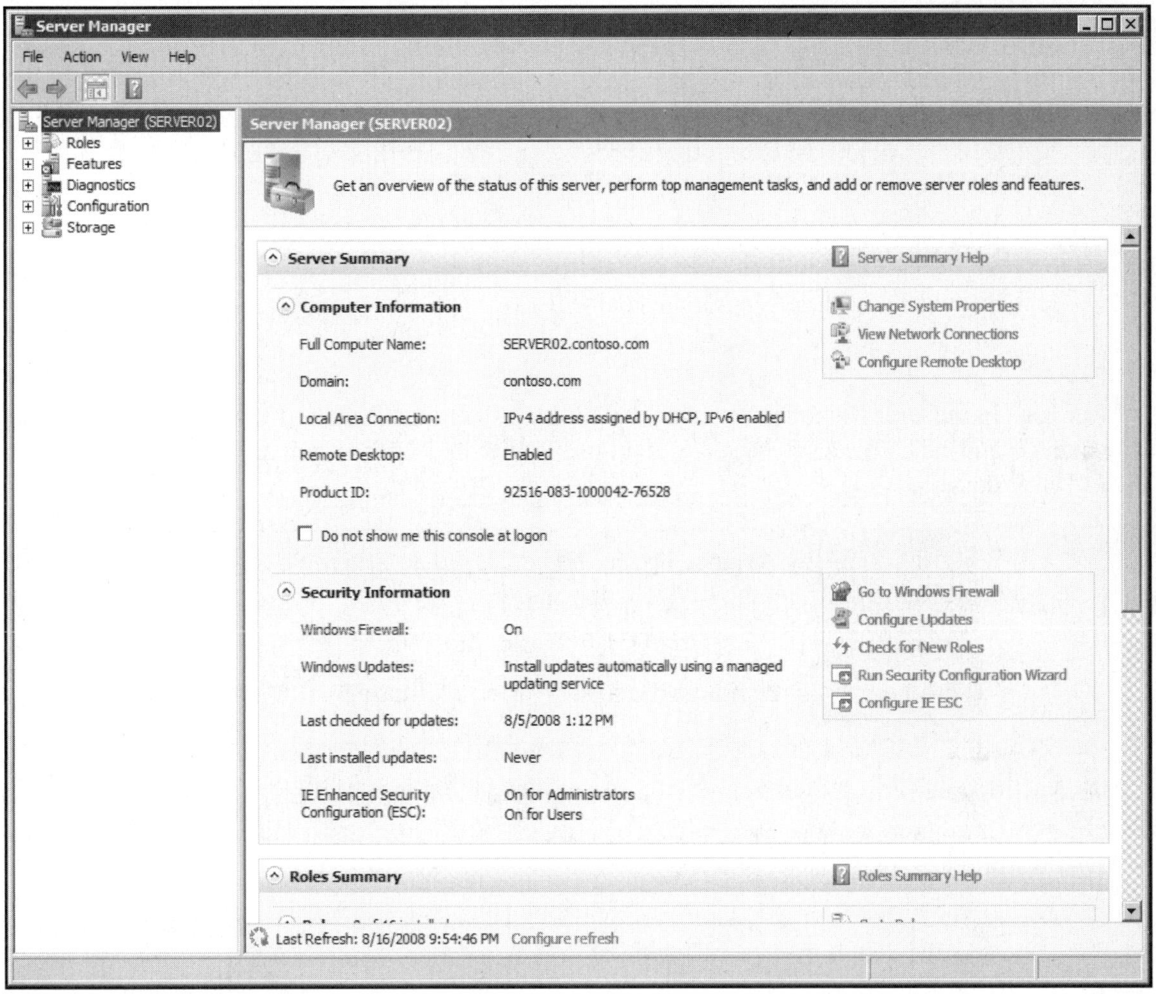

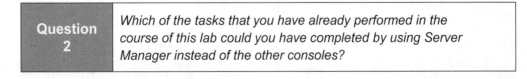

Figure 1-2
Server Manager console

Question 2	*Which of the tasks that you have already performed in the course of this lab could you have completed by using Server Manager instead of the other consoles?*

2. In the Server Summary section under Security Information, click Configure IE ESC. The Internet Explorer Enhanced Security Configuration dialog box appears.

3. Under Administrators, select the Off option, and click OK.

Question 3	Based on the information shown in the main Server Manager display, what roles are currently installed on the computer?

Question 4	What features are currently installed on the computer?

4. In the scope pane, select the Features node, and click Add Features. The Add Features Wizard appears, displaying the *Select Features* page.

5. Select the Group Policy Management checkbox.

6. Expand Remote Server Administration Tools and Role Administration Tools. Then, select the Active Directory Domain Services Tools checkbox, and click Next. The *Confirm Installation Selections* page appears.

7. Click Install. The wizard installs the features you selected.

8. Click Close. Restart the computer when the wizard prompts you to do so.

9. When the computer restarts, log on as Student##. The Server Manager console opens, and the Resume Configuration Wizard appears.

Question 5	What was the result of the installation?

10. Press Ctrl+Prt Scr to take a screen shot of the *Installation Results* page in the Resume Configuration Wizard, and then press Ctrl+V to paste the resulting image on the page provided in the lab01_worksheet file.

11. Click Close.

12. Leave Server Manager open for the next exercise.

NOTE	Completing the configuration tasks in Exercises 1.1 and 1.2 leaves the student computer in its baseline state, the state in which the computer is expected to be at the beginning of each subsequent lab in this manual.

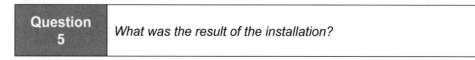

Exercise 1.3	Installing the Windows Deployment Services Role
Overview	One of the methods for deploying operating systems in Windows Server 2008 is Windows Deployment Services, which is provided as a role that you must install using the Server Manager console.
Completion time	10 minutes

1. In the Server Manager console, click the Roles node in the scope (left) pane.In the detail (right) pane, click Add Roles. The Add Roles Wizard appears.

2. Click Next to bypass the *Before You Begin* page. The *Select Server Roles* page appears, as shown in Figure 1-3.

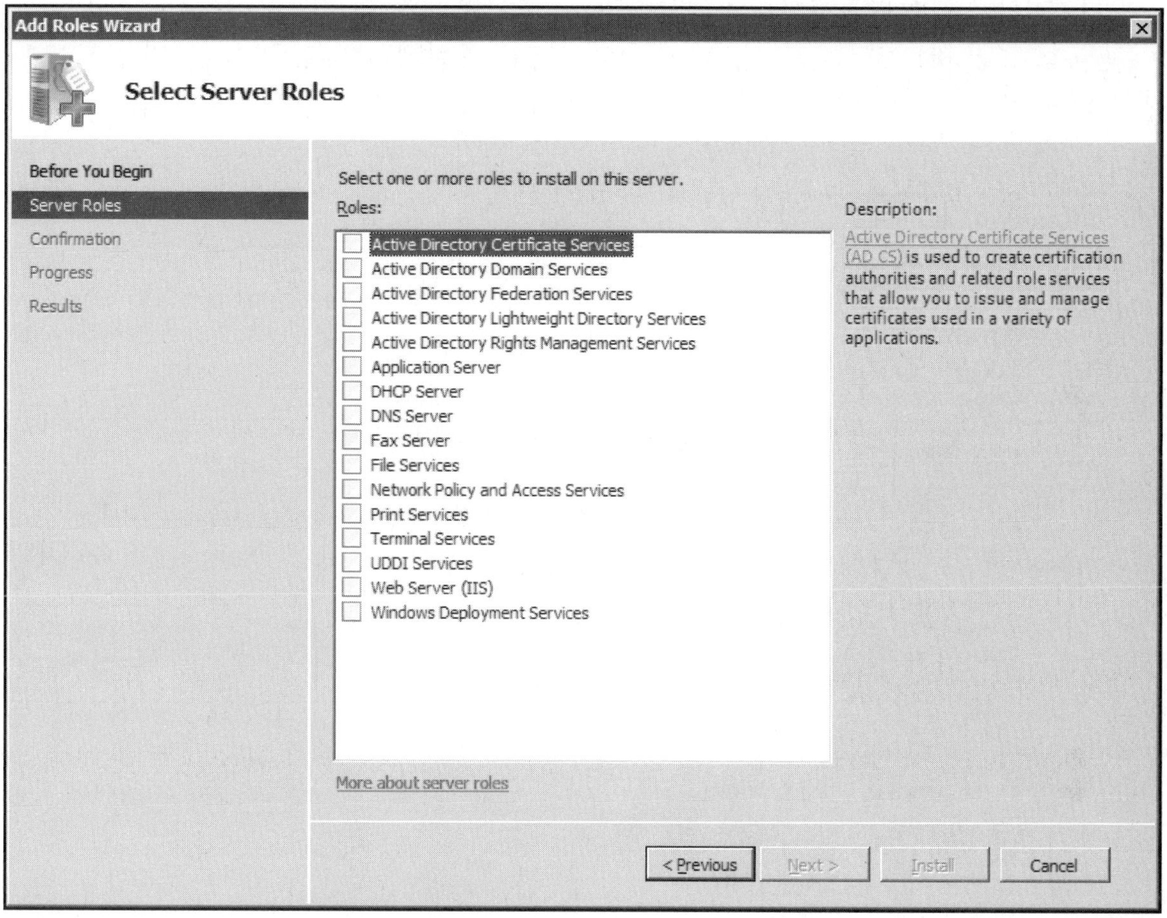

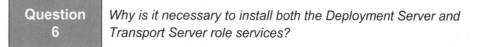

Figure 1-3
Select Server Roles page of the Add Roles Wizard

3. Select the Windows Deployment Services checkbox, and click Next. The *Overview of Windows Deployment Services* page appears.

4. Click Next. The *Select Role Services* page appears.

5. Leave the Deployment Server and Transport Server role services selected, and click Next. The *Confirm Installation Selections* page appears.

Question 6	Why is it necessary to install both the Deployment Server and Transport Server role services?

6. Click Install. The wizard installs the role.

7. Click Close.

8. Close the Server Manager console.

9. Leave the computer logged on for the next exercise.

Exercise 1.4	Configuring WDS
Overview	After you install Windows Deployment Services, it remains inactive until you configure the service and add the images that the server will deploy to clients. In this exercise, you configure basic WDS settings.
Completion time	10 minutes

1. Click Start, and then click Administrative Tools > Windows Deployment Services. Click Continue in the User Account Control message box. The Windows Deployment Services console appears, as shown in Figure 1-4.

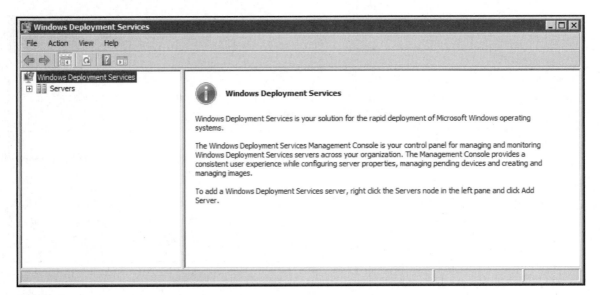

Figure 1-4
Windows Deployment Services console

2. In the scope (left) pane, expand the Servers node. Right-click your server (Server##.contoso.com) and, from the context menu, select Configure Server. The Windows Deployment Services Configuration Wizard appears.

3. Click Next to bypass the Welcome page. The *Remote Installation Folder Location* page appears.

4. In the Path text box, key **C:\Images**, and click Next. A System Volume Warning message box appears, reminding you that the remote installation folder should not be located on the system volume. It is acceptable in a lab environment, however, so click Yes to continue. The *PXE Server Initial Settings* page appears.

5. Select the Respond to all (known and unknown) client computers option, and click Finish. The wizard configures Windows Deployment Services, and the *Configuration Complete* page appears.

Question 7	*Why would an administrator want to select the Respond only to known client computers option on the PXE Server Initial Settings page?*

6. Clear the Add Images To The Windows Deployment Server Now checkbox, and click Finish. The wizard closes.

7. Press Ctrl+Prt Scr to take a screen shot of the configured Windows Deployment Services console, and then press Ctrl+V to paste the resulting image on the page provided in the lab01_worksheet file.

8. Leave the Windows Deployment Services console open for the next exercise.

Exercise 1.5	Adding Images
Overview	Before you can deploy images to client computers using WDS, you must add them to the WDS console. In this exercise, you add boot and install image files to the console using the images supplied on the Windows Server 2008 installation disk.
Completion time	10 minutes

1. In the Windows Deployment Services console, expand the node for your server. Then, right-click the Boot Images folder and, from the context menu, select Add Boot Image. The Windows Deployment Services – Add Image Wizard appears, showing the *Image File* page, as shown in Figure 1-5.

2. In the File location text box, key **\\serverdc\install\WinSvr2008\sources\boot.wim**, and click Next. The *Image Metadata* page appears.

3. In the Image Name text box, key **Windows Server 2008 Setup (x86)** or **Windows Server 2008 (x64)**, depending on which version you are using, and then click Next. The *Summary* page appears.

4. Click Next. The wizard adds the boot image to the store.

5. When the process is completed, click Finish. The boot image appears in the console.

6. Back in the console, right-click the Install Images folder. From the context menu, select Add Install Image. The Windows Deployment Services – Add Image Wizard appears, showing the *Image Group* page.

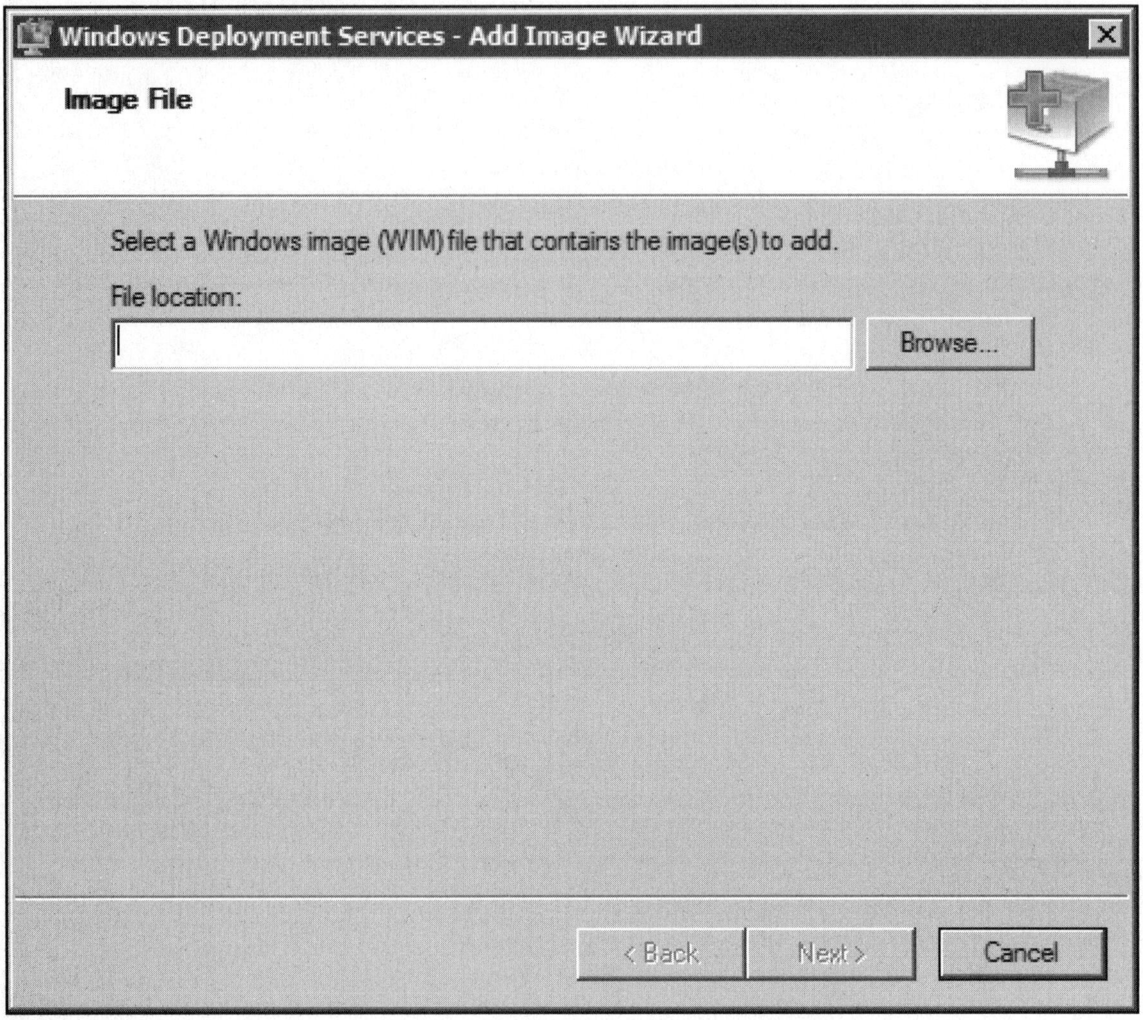

Figure 1-5
Image File page in the Windows Deployment Services – Add Image Wizard

7. In the Create a new image group text box, key **Windows Server 2008**, and then click Next. The *Image File* page appears.

8. In the File location text box, key **\\serverdc\install\WinSvr2008\sources\install.wim**, and click Next. The *List of Available Images* page appears.

9. Clear all of the image checkboxes except Windows Longhorn SERVERENTERPRISE (or SERVERENTERPRISEV if you are using a non–Hyper-V version of Windows Server 2008), and click Next. The *Summary* page appears.

10. Click Next. The wizard adds the install image to the store.

11. When the process is completed, click Finish. The boot image appears in the console.

12. Press Ctrl+Prt Scr to take a screen shot of the Windows Deployment Services console displaying the install image, and then press Ctrl+V to paste the resulting image on the page provided in the lab01_worksheet file.

13. Close the Windows Deployment Services console.

14. Leave the computer logged on for the next exercise.

Exercise 1.6	Installing Windows Automated Installation Kit
Overview	Windows Server 2008 does not ship with the Windows Automated Installation Kit; it is a separate download. Your instructor has made this software available to you on the classroom server. In this exercise, you install the Windows AIK software.
Completion time	10 minutes

1. Click Start, and then click Run. The Run dialog box appears.

2. In the Open text box, key **\\serverdc\install\WindowsAIK\startcd.exe**, and click OK. The *Welcome to Windows Automated Installation Kit* window appears, as shown in Figure 1-6.

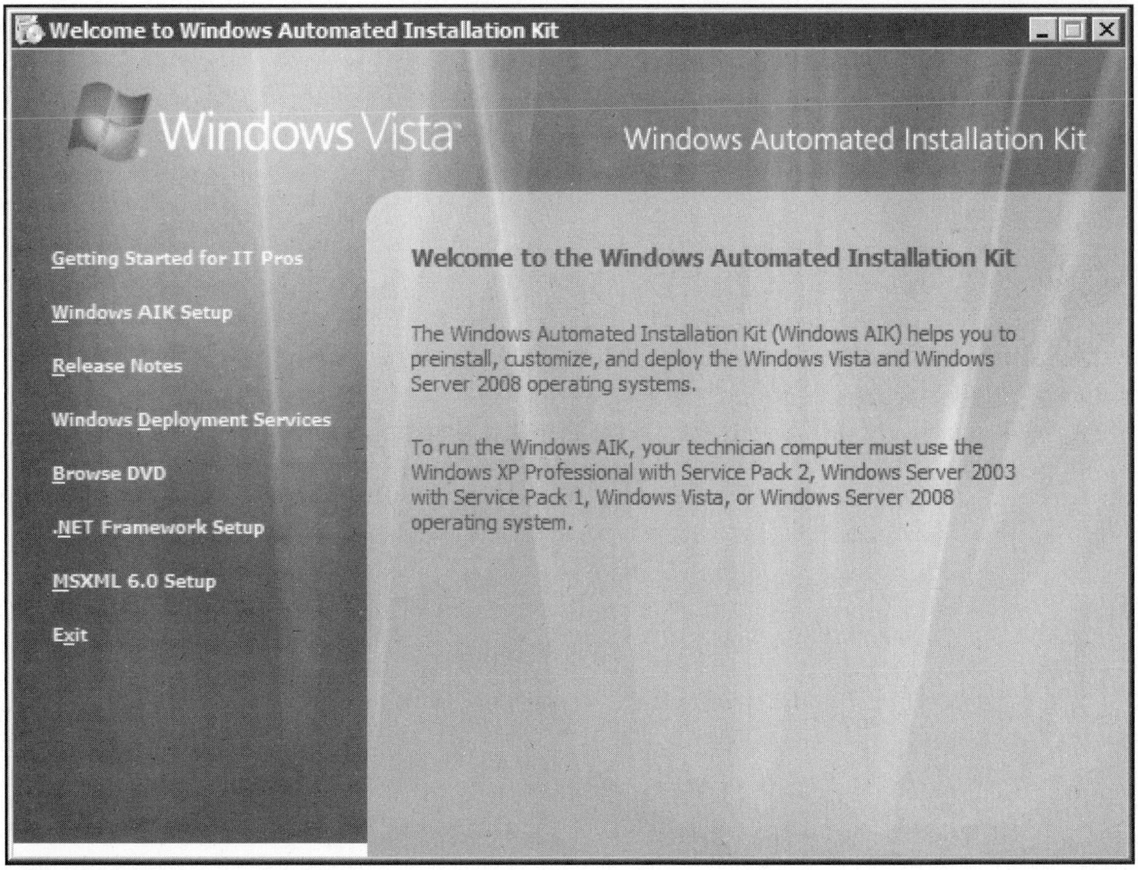

Figure 1-6
Welcome to Windows Automated Installation Kit window

3. Click Windows AIK Setup. The Windows Automated Installation Kit Setup Wizard appears.

4. Click Next to bypass the Welcome page. The *License Terms* page appears.

5. Select I Agree, and then click Next. The *Select Installation Folder* page appears.

6. Click Next to accept the default settings. The *Confirm Installation* page appears.

7. Click Next. The wizard installs the Windows AIK, and the *Installation Complete* page appears.

8. Click Close. The wizard closes.

9. Close the Welcome to Windows Automated Installation Kit window.

Exercise 1.7	Using Windows System Image Manager
Overview	Windows Server Image Manager is the Windows AIK graphical tool that you use to create the answer files that enable you to perform unattended operating system installations. In this exercise, you use Windows System Image Manager to create a sample answer file.
Completion time	20 minutes

1. Click Start, and then click All Programs > Accessories > Command Prompt. A Command Prompt window appears.

2. In the Command Prompt window, key **copy \\serverdc\install\WinSvr2008\sources\install.wim c:\images**, and press Enter.

3. When the copy process is completed (which can take several minutes), close the Command Prompt window.

4. Click Start, and then click All Programs > Microsoft Windows AIK > Windows System Image Manager. The Windows System Image Manager window appears, as shown in Figure 1-7.

5. Click File > Select Windows Image. The Select a Windows Image combo box appears.

6. Browse to the C:\Images folder, select the Install.wim file you copied there, and click Open. The Select an Image dialog box appears.

7. Select the Windows Longhorn SERVERENTERPRISE entry, and click OK. A Windows System Image Manager message box appears, prompting you to create a catalog file.

8. Click Yes, and then click Continue in the User Account Control message box. The program adds the image you selected to the Windows Image pane.

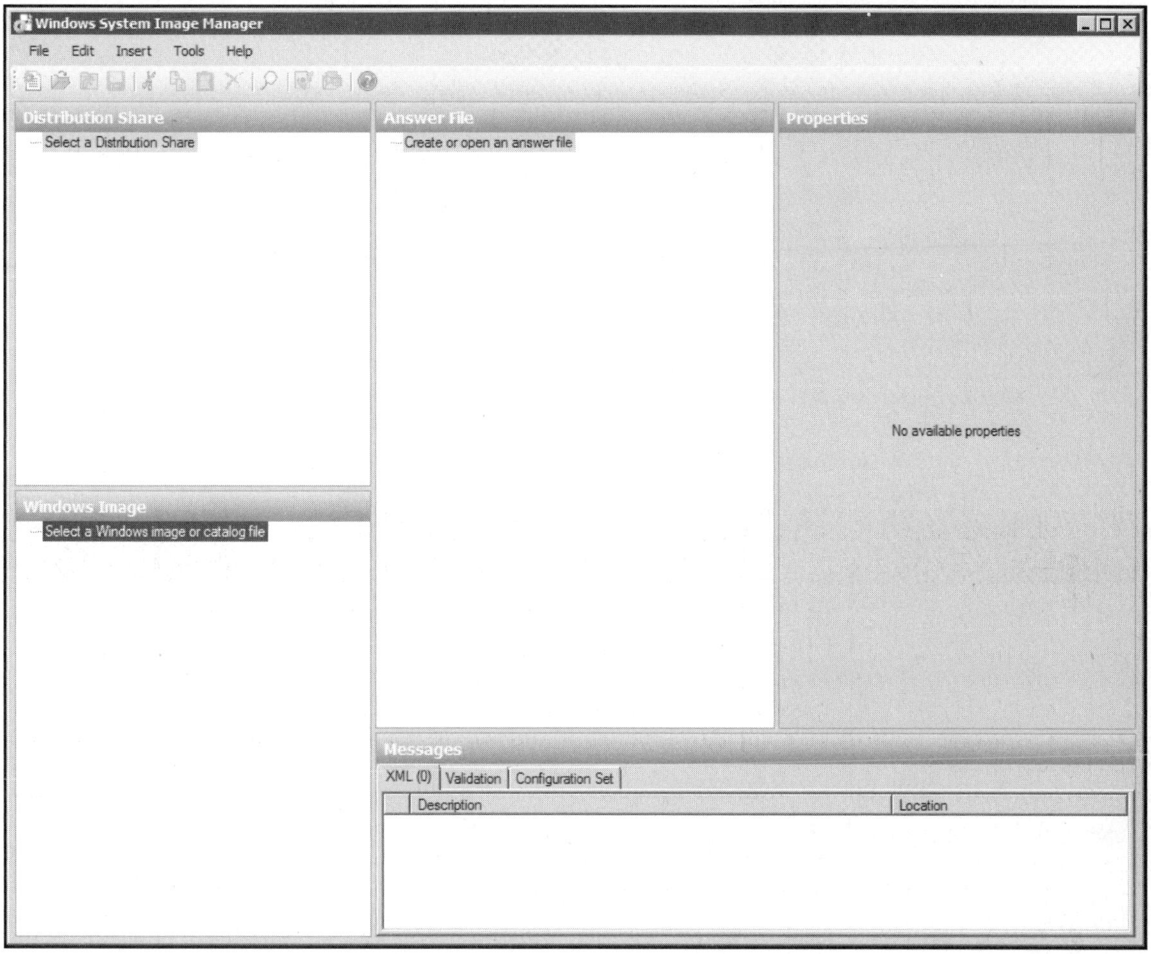

Figure 1-7
Windows System Image Manager window

9. Click File > New Answer File. A list of components appears in the Answer File pane.

10. In the Windows Image pane, browse to the Windows Longhorn SERVERENTERPRISE > Components > x86_Microsoft-Windows-Setup_6.0.6001.18000_neutral > Disk Configuration node. Right-click the Disk node and, from the context menu, select Add Setting to Pass 1 windowsPE. The component you selected appears in the Answer File pane.

> **NOTE**
>
> *If you are using a 64-bit version of Windows Server 2008, component names use x64 instead of x86.*

11. In the Answer File pane, select the Disk node.

12. In the Disk Properties pane, select DiskID.

13. In the value box for DiskID setting, key **0**.

14. In the Disk Properties pane, select WillWipeDisk.

15. In the WillWipeDisk drop-down list, select True.

Question 8	What will the WillWipeDisk setting do when added to an answer file and activated?

16. In the Windows Image pane, expand the Disk node, and add the CreatePartition setting to the answer file.

17. In the Answer File pane, configure the CreatePartition setting to create a 20-GB primary partition.

Question 9	What CreatePartition settings did you configure, and what values did you assign to them?

18. Add the settings in Table 1-1 to the answer file, and configure them as specified.

Table 1-1
Answer File Settings for Windows System Image Manager

Component	Node	Setting	Add To	Value
x86_Microsoft-Windows-Setup_6.0.6001.18000_neutral	User Data	AcceptEULA	Pass 1 windowsPE	True
x86_Microsoft-Windows-Setup_6.0.6001.18000_neutral	User Data	FullName	Pass 1 windowsPE	Your Name
x86_Microsoft-Windows-Setup_6.0.6001.18000_neutral	User Data	Organization	Pass 1 windowsPE	Your School's Name
x86_Microsoft-Windows-Shell-Setup_6.0.6001.18000_neutral	N/A	ComputerName	Pass 4 specialize	Server##
x86_Microsoft-Windows-Shell-Setup_6.0.6001.18000_neutral	User Accounts	AdministratorPassword	Pass 7 oobeSystem	P@ssw0rd
x86_Microsoft-Windows-DNS-Client_6.0.6001.18000_neutral	N/A	DNSDomain	Pass 4 specialize	Contoso.com

19. Click Tools > Validate Answer File.

Question 10	What results are shown in the Messages pane?

20. Press Ctrl+Prt Scr to take a screen shot of the Windows System Image Manager window, and then press Ctrl+V to paste the resulting image on the page provided in the lab01_worksheet file.

21. Click File > Save Answer File As. The Save As combo box appears.

22. Save the answer file to your computer's Student##\Documents folder, giving it the name Student##_answer_file.xml.

23. Close the Windows System Image Manager window.

24. Log off of the computer.

LAB REVIEW QUESTIONS

Completion time	10 minutes

1. In Exercise 1.5, you added a boot image to the Windows Deployment Services console. Describe how a computer on the same network as the WDS server can boot using that image.

2. What two basic methods capture an image of a Windows Server 2008 computer by using the tools you installed in this lab?

LAB CHALLENGE: CAPTURING AN IMAGE

Completion time	30 minutes

Your instructor will supply you with a Windows PE boot disk. To complete this challenge, boot your system from the disk, and capture an image of your computer to a file named Student##_image.wim on the system's local drive. Using only tools on the boot disk, map a drive to the \\ServerDC\Students share, and copy the image file to the Student## folder on that share.

WORKSTATION RESET: RETURNING TO BASELINE

Completion time	10 minutes

To return the computer to its baseline state, complete the following procedures.

1. Open the Server Manager console, and remove the Windows Deployment Services role you installed during the course of the lab.

2. Restart the computer.

LAB 2
DEPLOYING INFRASTRUCTURE SERVICES

This lab contains the following exercises and activities:

Exercise 2.1	Designing a DNS Namespace
Exercise 2.2	Installing the DNS Server Role
Exercise 2.3	Creating a Zone
Exercise 2.4	Creating Domains
Exercise 2.5	Creating Resource Records
Exercise 2.6	Installing the DHCP Role
Exercise 2.7	Creating a Scope
Lab Review	Questions
Lab Challenge	Using Reverse Name Resolution
Workstation Reset	Returning to Baseline

BEFORE YOU BEGIN

The classroom network consists of Windows Server 2008 student servers that are all connected to a local area network. There is also a classroom server, named ServerDC, that is

connected to the same classroom network. ServerDC is also running Windows Server 2008 and is the domain controller for a domain named contoso.com. Throughout the labs in this manual, you will be working with the same student server on which you will install, configure, maintain, and troubleshoot application roles, features, and services.

Your instructor should have supplied you with the information needed to fill in the following table:

Student computer name (Server##)	
Student account name (Student##)	

Working with Lab Worksheets

Each lab in this manual requires that you answer questions, shoot screen shots, or perform other activities that you are to document in a worksheet named for the lab, such as lab01_worksheet. Your instructor will supply you with the worksheet files by copying them to the Students\Worksheets share on ServerDC. As you perform the exercises in each lab, open the appropriate worksheet file using WordPad, fill in the required information, and save the file to your computer's Student##\Documents folder. This folder is automatically redirected to the ServerDC computer. Your instructor will examine these worksheet files to assess your performance.

The procedure for opening and saving a worksheet file is as follows:

1. Click Start, and then click Run. The Run dialog box appears.

2. In the Open text box, key **\\ServerDC\Students\Worksheets\lab##_worksheet** (where lab## contains the number of the lab you're completing), and click OK.

3. The worksheet document opens in Wordpad.

4. Complete all of the exercises in the worksheet.

5. In WordPad, choose Save As from the File menu. The Save As dialog box appears.

6. In the File Name text box, key **lab##_worksheet_*yourname*** (where lab## contains the number of the lab you're completing and *yourname* is your last name), and click Save.

SCENARIO

You are a newly hired administrator for Contoso, Ltd., assigned to work in the company's testing lab. The company will be introducing a new division in the near future, and you have been told to create test implementations of the Windows Server 2008 infrastructure services that the new division will need.

After completing this lab, you will be able to:

- Install and configure a DNS server

- Install and configure a DHCP server

Estimated lab time: 125 minutes

Exercise 2.1	Designing a DNS Namespace
Overview	The new division will have its own DNS namespace, and your first task is to design that namespace by specifying appropriate domain and host names for the computers in the division.
Completion time	15 minutes

1. Design a DNS namespace for your organization that conforms to the following guidelines.

    a. The root domain name for the organization is adatum##.com, where ## is the number assigned to your computer by your instructor. All of the additional domains that you create must be subordinate to this domain.

    b. The internal network must be located in a different domain from the external network.

    c. The organization consists of three internal divisions: Sales, Human Resources, and Production. Each division must be represented by a separate subdomain in the namespace.

    d. Each division has departmental servers performing various roles and as many as 200 workstations, only some of which are shown in the diagram. Your host names should identify the function of each computer.

    e. Three servers on an external perimeter network host the company's Internet services: Web, FTP, and e-mail. These servers must be in the domain adatum##.com.

2. In the diagram provided in Figure 2-1 on the following page, write both the domain names and the fully qualified domain names that you have selected for the computers in the appropriate spaces.

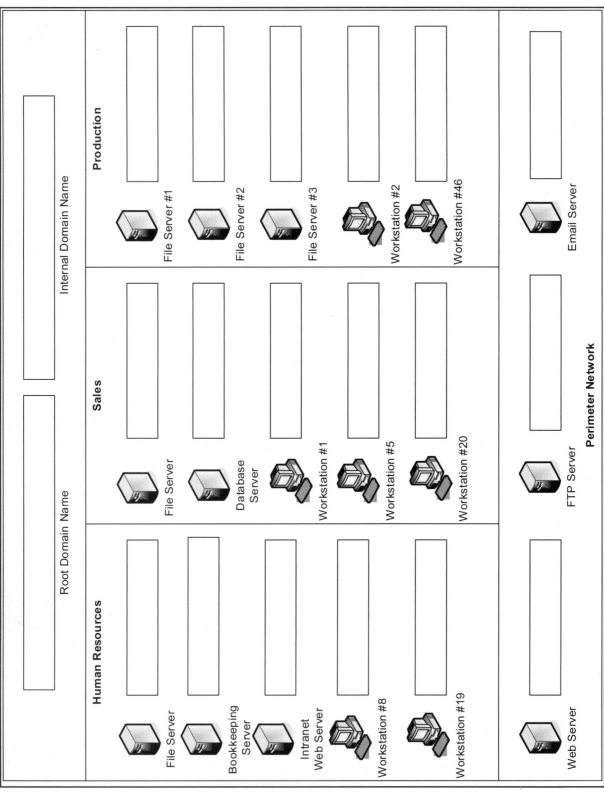

Figure 2-1
Server Manager console

Exercise 2.2	**Installing the DNS Server Role**
Overview	To deploy the DNS namespace you designed in Exercise 2.1, you must first install the DNS Server role on a Windows Server 2008 computer.
Completion time	10 minutes

1. Turn on your computer. When the logon screen appears, log on to the domain with your Student## account, where## is the number assigned by your instructor, using the password *P@ssw0rd*.

2. Click Start, point to Administrative Tools, and click Server Manager. Click Continue in the User Account Control message box, and the Server Manager console appears.

3. Select the Roles node, and click Add Roles. The Add Roles Wizard appears, displaying the *Before You Begin* page.

4. Click Next to continue. The *Select Server Roles* page appears.

5. Select the DNS Server role. A message box appears, warning that the computer does not have a static IP address.

6. Click Install DNS Server anyway, and then click Next. The *DNS Server* page appears.

7. Click Next to continue. The *Confirm Installation Selections* page appears.

8. Click Install. The wizard installs the DNS Server role.

9. Click Close.

10. Close the Server Manager console.

11. Leave the computer logged on for the next exercise.

Exercise 2.3	**Creating a Zone**
Overview	A zone is the administrative division that DNS servers use to administer domains. The first step in implementing the DNS namspace that you designed is to create a zone representing your root domain.
Completion time	10 minutes

1. Click Start, and then click Administrative Tools > DNS. Click Continue in the User Account Control message box, and the DNS Manager console appears.

2. Expand the SERVER## node, as shown in Figure 2-2.

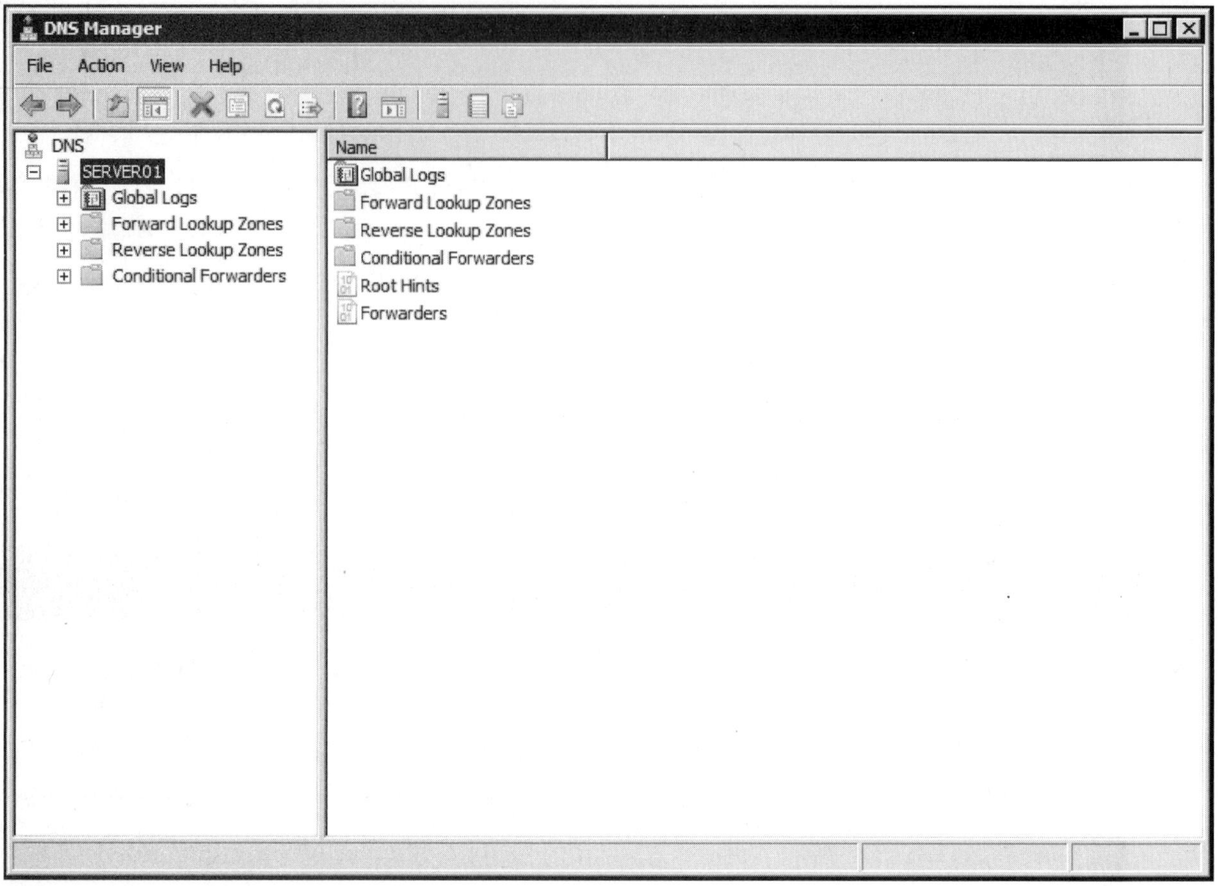

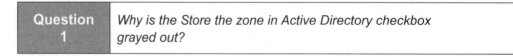

Figure 2-2
DNS Manager console

3. Right-click the Forward Lookup Zones folder and, from the context menu, select New Zone. The New Zone Wizard appears.

> **NOTE**
>
> *Because the domains you specified in your DNS namespace design are completely separate from the contoso.com domain used for your classroom network, the zones and other elements you create in this lab will not interfere with the name resolution process on your computers.*

4. Click Next to bypass the Welcome page. The *Zone Type* page appears.

> | **Question 1** | *Why is the Store the zone in Active Directory checkbox grayed out?* |
> | --- | --- |

5. Leave the Primary Zone option selected, and click Next. The *Zone Name* page appears.

6. In the Zone name text box, key the root domain name from the diagram you created in Exercise 2.1, and click Next. The *Zone File* page appears.

7. Click Next to accept the default zone file name. The *Dynamic Update* page appears.

8. Select the Allow both nonsecure and secure dynamic updates option, and click Next. The *Completing the New Zone Wizard* page appears.

9. Click Finish. The new zone appears in the Forward Lookup Zones folder in the console.

Question 2	*What resource records appear in the new zone you created by default?*

10. Repeat steps 3 to 9 to create another zone by using the internal domain name you specified in the diagram in Exercise 2.1.

11. Leave the DNS Manager console open for the next exercise.

Exercise 2.4	Creating Domains
Overview	A single zone on a DNS server can encompass multiple domains as long as the domains are contiguous. In this exercise, you create the departmental domains you specified in your namespace design.
Completion time	5 minutes

1. In the DNS Manager console, right-click the zone you created using the internal domain name from your namespace in Exercise 2.3. From the context menu, select New Domain. The New DNS Domain dialog box appears, as shown in Figure 2-3.

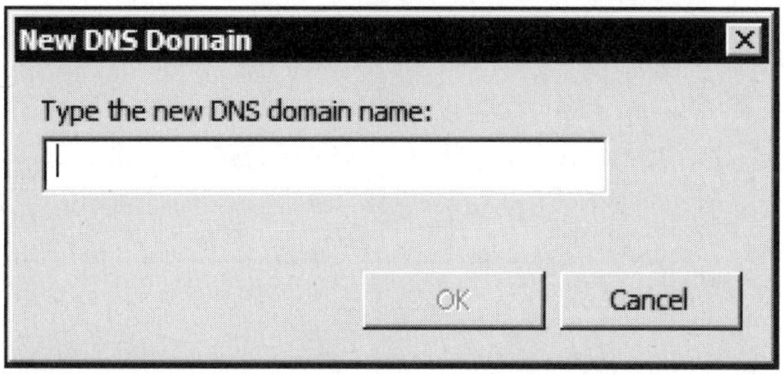

Figure 2-3
New DNS Domain dialog box

2. In the Type the new DNS domain name text box, key the name of the Human Resources domain you specified in your namespace design, and click OK.

NOTE	*When you create a domain within a zone, you specify the name for the new domain relative to the zone name. For example, to create the qa.contoso.com domain in the contoso.com zone, you would specify only the qa name in the New DNS Domain dialog box.*

3. Repeat steps 1 to 2 to create the domains for the Sales and Production departments from your namespace design.

Question 3	What resource records appear in the new domains you created by default?

4. Leave the DNS Manager console open for the next exercise.

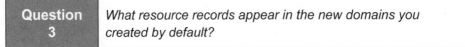

Exercise 2.5	Creating Resource Records
Overview	Now that you have created the zones and domains for your namespace, you can begin to populate them with the resource records that the DNS server uses to resolve host names into IP addresses.
Completion time	15 minutes

1. In the DNS Manager console, right-click the root domain zone you created in Exercise 2.3. From the context menu, select New Host (A or AAAA). The New Host dialog box appears, as shown in Figure 2-4.

2. In the Name text box, key the host name of the Internet Web server you specified in your namespace design.

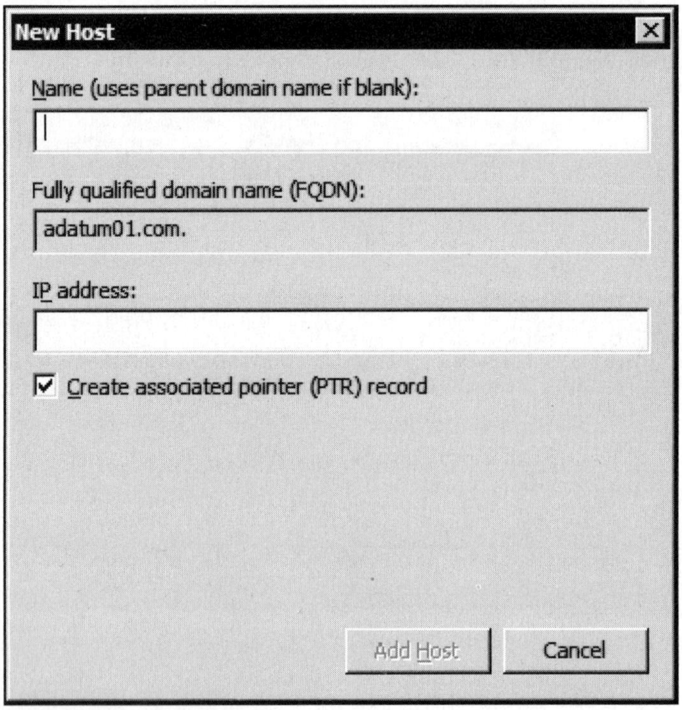

New Host ☒

Name (uses parent domain name if blank):

[   ]

Fully qualified domain name (FQDN):

adatum01.com.

IP address:

[   ]

☑ Create associated pointer (PTR) record

Add Host   Cancel

Figure 2-4
New Host dialog box

3. In the IP Address text box, key **10.1.*xx*.201**, where *xx* is the number assigned to your computer by your instructor, omitting any leading zeroes. For example, you can use 10.1.3.201, but not 10.1.03.201.

4. Click Add Host. A DNS message box appears, stating that the resource record was created.

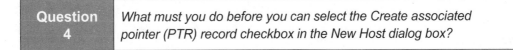

Question 4	*What must you do before you can select the Create associated pointer (PTR) record checkbox in the New Host dialog box?*

5. Click OK. A new, blank Add Host dialog box appears.

6. Repeat steps 2 to 4 to create Host records for the Internet FTP and e-mail servers in your namespace design. For each resource record, use a different IP address on the 10.1.*xx* subnet.

7. In the three domains you created in Exercise 2.4, create Host resource records for all of the remaining computers in your namespace design, using the names you specified in your diagram and a different IP address in the 10.1.*xx* subnet for each record.

> *For the purposes of this exercise, the actual IP addresses you use when creating your resource records do not matter. In an actual DNS deployment, you must either specify an appropriate IP address for each host, based on the subnet to which the computer is connected, or rely on DHCP to create the resource records for the computers.*

8. Click Done to close the Add Host dialog box.

9. Press Ctrl+Prt Scr to take a screen shot of the DNS Manager console, showing the resource records you created in the Human Resources domain, and then press Ctrl+V to paste the resulting image into the lab02_worksheet file in the page provided.

10. Close the DNS Manager console.

Exercise 2.6	Installing the DHCP Role
Overview	DHCP enables computers on the lab network to obtain their own IP addresses and other critical TCP/IP settings. To deploy a DHCP server, you must first install the DHCP role using Server Manager.
Completion time	15 minutes

1. Click Start, point to Administrative Tools, and click Server Manager. Click Continue in the User Account Control message box, and the Server Manager console appears.

2. Select the Roles node, and click Add Roles. The Add Roles Wizard appears, displaying the *Before You Begin* page.

3. Click Next to continue. The *Select Server Roles* page appears.

4. Select the DHCP Server role. A message box appears, warning that the computer does not have a static IP address.

5. Click Install DHCP Server anyway.

6. Click Next to continue. The *DHCP Server* page appears.

7. Click Next. The *Specify IPv4 DNS Server Settings* page appears.

8. In the Parent Domain text box, key the root domain name you specified in your DNS namespace design in Exercise 2.1.

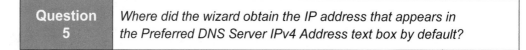

Question 5	Where did the wizard obtain the IP address that appears in the Preferred DNS Server IPv4 Address text box by default?

9. Click the Validate button.

Question 6	What happens?

10. Press Ctrl+Prt Scr to take a screen shot of the Add Roles Wizard, showing the *Specify IPv4 DNS Server Settings* page, and then press Ctrl+V to paste the resulting image into the lab02_worksheet file in the page provided.

11. Click Next to continue. The *Specify IPv4 WINS Server Settings* page appears.

12. Click Next to accept the default settings. The *DHCP Scopes* page appears.

13. Click Next to continue. The *Configure DHCPv6 Stateless Mode* page appears.

14. Select the Disable DHCPv6 stateless mode for the server option and click Next. The *Authorize DHCP Server* page appears.

15. Select the Skip authorization of this DHCP server in AD DS option and click Next. The *Confirm Installation Selections* page appears.

16. Click Install. The wizard installs the DHCP Server role.

17. Click Close. The wizard closes.

18. Close the Server Manager console.

19. Leave the computer logged on for the next exercise.

Exercise 2.7	**Creating a Scope**
Overview	A scope is a range of IP addresses that a DHCP server uses to supply clients on a particular subnet with IP addresses. In this exercise, you create a scope on your DHCP server.
Completion time	15 minutes

1. Click Start, point to Administrative Tools, and click DHCP. Click Continue in the User Account Control message box, and the DHCP console appears, as shown in Figure 2-5.

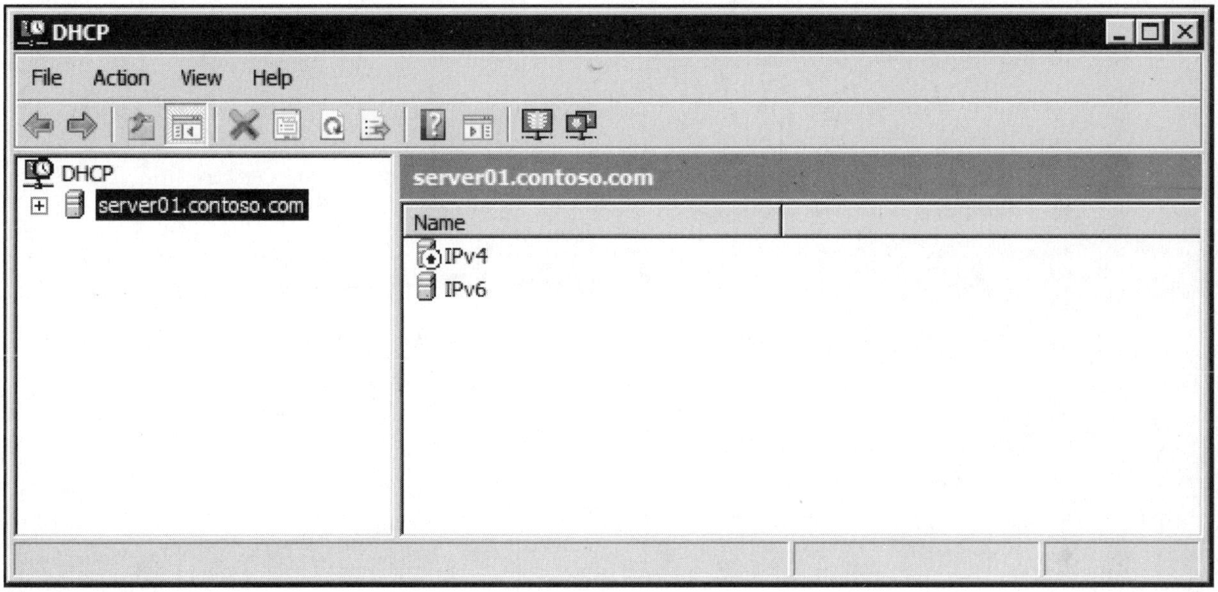

Figure 2-5
DHCP console

2. Expand the server##.contoso.com node.

3. Right-click the IPv4 node and, from the context menu, select New Scope. The New Scope Wizard appears.

4. Click Next to bypass the Welcome page. The *Scope Name* page appears.

5. In the Name text box, key **Student## Scope**, and click Next. The *IP Address Range* page appears.

6. In the Start IP address text box, key **10.1.##.240**, where ## is the number assigned to your computer by your instructor, omitting any leading zeroes.

7. In the End IP address text box, key **10.1.##.250**.

Question 7	Notice that the wizard automatically adds a value to the Subnet mask text box. Where did this value come from?

8. In the Subnet mask text box, key **255.255.255.0**, and then click Next. The *Add Exclusions* page appears.

9. In the Start IP address text box, key **10.1.##.245**.

10. In the End IP address text box, key **10.1.##.245**.

11. Click Add. The address appears in the Excluded address range list.

12. Click Next. The *Lease Duration* page appears.

13. Click Next to accept the default value. The *Configure DHCP Options* page appears.

14. Click Next to accept the Yes, I want to configure these options now option. The *Router (Default Gateway)* page appears.

15. In the IP address text box, key **10.1.1.100** and then click Add.

16. Click Next to continue. The *Domain Name and DNS Servers* page appears.

17. In the Parent domain text box, key the name of the root domain you specified in your namespace design in Exercise 2.1.

18. In the Server name text box, key **Server##**, where ## is the number assigned to your computer by your instructor, and click Resolve. Your computer's IP address appears in the adjacent text box.

19. Click Add, and then click Next. The *WINS Servers* page appears.

20. Click Next to bypass the page. The *Activate Scope* page appears.

21. Click Next to accept the default Yes, I Want To Activate This Scope Now option. The *Completing the New Scope Wizard* page appears.

22. Click Finish. The scope is added to the console.

23. Expand the IPv4 node and the new scope, and then select the Address Pool folder.

24. Press Ctrl+Prt Scr to take a screen shot of the DHCP console, showing the contents of the Address Pool folder, and then press Ctrl+V to paste the resulting image into the lab02_worksheet file in the page provided.

25. Close the DHCP console, and log off of the computer.

LAB REVIEW QUESTIONS

Completion time	10 minutes

1. In Exercise 2.3, which of the *New Zone Wizard* pages would not appear if you opted to store your zones in Active Directory?

2. In Exercise 2.6, why would the lack of a static IP address be a problem, considering that DHCP clients use broadcast transmissions to locate DHCP servers?

3. The Windows DHCP server enables you to configure DHCP options at the scope level—affecting only the clients obtaining addresses from that scope—and at the server level, affecting clients obtaining addresses from any scope on the server. On an actual production network, why would it be more practical to configure the Router option as a scope option and the DNS Servers option as a server option?

LAB CHALLENGE: USING REVERSE NAME RESOLUTION

Completion time	20 minutes

Reverse name resolution occurs when a resolver sends an IP address to a DNS server and receives a host name in return rather than sending a host name and receiving an IP address. To complete this challenge, you must configure your DNS server to perform reverse name resolutions for all of the resource records you created in Exercise 2.5.

1. List the basic tasks you performed to complete the challenge.

2. Press Ctrl+Prt Scr to take a screen shot of the DNS Manager console, showing the elements you created during the challenge, and then press Ctrl+V to paste the resulting image into the lab02_worksheet file in the page provided.

WORKSTATION RESET: RETURNING TO BASELINE

Completion time	10 minutes

To return the computer to its baseline state, complete the following procedures.

1. Open the Server Manager console.

2. Remove the DNS Server and DHCP Server roles you installed during the course of the lab. Restart the computer.

LAB 3
DEPLOYING ACTIVE DIRECTORY

This lab contains the following exercises and activities:

BEFORE YOU BEGIN

The classroom network consists of Windows Server 2008 student servers that are all connected to a local area network. There is also a classroom server, named ServerDC, that is connected to the same classroom network. ServerDC is also running Windows Server 2008 and is the domain controller for a domain named contoso.com. Throughout the labs in this manual, you will be working with the same student server on which you will install, configure, maintain, and troubleshoot application roles, features, and services.

Your instructor should have supplied you with the information needed to fill in the following table:

Student computer name (Server##)	
Student account name (Student##)	

Working with Lab Worksheets

Each lab in this manual requires that you answer questions, shoot screen shots, or perform other activities that you are to document in a worksheet named for the lab, such as lab01_worksheet. Your instructor will supply you with the worksheet files by copying them to the Students\Worksheets share on ServerDC. As you perform the exercises in each lab, open the appropriate worksheet file using WordPad, fill in the required information, and save the file to your computer's Student##\Documents folder. This folder is automatically redirected to the ServerDC computer. Your instructor will examine these worksheet files to assess your performance.

The procedure for opening and saving a worksheet file is as follows:

1. Click Start, and then click Run. The Run dialog box appears.

2. In the Open text box, key **\\ServerDC\Students\Worksheets\lab##_worksheet** (where lab## contains the number of the lab you're completing), and click OK.

3. The worksheet document opens in Wordpad.

4. Complete all of the exercises in the worksheet.

5. In WordPad, choose Save As from the File menu. The Save As dialog box appears.

6. In the File Name text box, key **lab##_worksheet_*yourname*** (where lab## contains the number of the lab you're completing and *yourname* is your last name), and click Save.

During sections of this lab, you will be changing your computer's domain affiliation, and the ServerDC computer will not be accessible. During these times, you can save the worksheet file to a local folder and copy it to your Student##\Documents folder at the end of the exercise.

SCENARIO

You are a newly hired administrator for Contoso, Ltd., assigned to work in the company's testing lab. The company will be introducing a new division in the near future, and you are testing various ways of integrating the division into the company's Active Directory namespace.

After completing this lab, you will be able to:

- Install the Active Directory Domain Services role

- Create a subdomain

- Create a new forest

Estimated lab time: 130 minutes

Exercise 3.1	Installing Active Directory Domain Services
Overview	The IT director has decided that the new division should have its own domain, and your first assignment is to build the domain controller for that domain on a Windows Server 2008 computer. In this exercise, you install the Active Directory Domain Services role.
Completion time	5 minutes

1. Turn on your computer. When the logon screen appears, log on to the domain with your Student## account, where ## is the number assigned by your instructor, using the password *P@ssw0rd*.

2. Click Start, point to Administrative Tools, and click Server Manager. Click Continue in the User Account Control message box, and the Server Manager console appears.

3. Select the Roles node, and click Add Roles. The Add Roles Wizard appears, displaying the *Before You Begin* page.

4. Click Next to continue. The *Select Server Roles* page appears.

5. Select the Active Directory Domain Services role, and click Next. The *Active Directory Domain Services* page appears.

6. Click Next to continue. The *Confirm Installation Selections* page appears.

7. Click Install. The wizard installs the role.

8. Click Close. The wizard closes.

9. Close the Server Manager console.

10. Leave the computer logged on for the next exercise.

Exercise 3.2	Creating a New Subdomain
Overview	The first domain configuration you have been instructed to test is a subdomain beneath the company's existing contoso.com domain. In this exercise, you create the new subdomain by promoting your server to a domain controller.
Completion time	15 minutes

1. Click Start, and then click Run. The Run dialog box appears.

2. In the Open text box, key **dcpromo.exe**, and click OK. Click Continue in the User Account Control message box. The Active Directory Domain Services Installation Wizard appears, displaying the Welcome page, as shown in Figure 3-1.

Figure 3-1
Active Directory Domain Services Installation Wizard

3. Select the Use advanced mode installation checkbox, and click Next. The *Operating System Compatibility* page appears.

4. Click Next to continue. The *Choose a Deployment Configuration* page appears.

5. Select the Existing Forest option. Select the Create a new domain in an existing forest option, and then click Next. The *Network Credentials* page appears.

6. Click Next to accept the default settings. The *Name The New Domain* page appears.

7. In the Single-label DNS name of the child domain text box, key **domain##**, where ## is the number assigned to your computer.

Question 1	What is the fully qualified domain name (FQDN) of the new domain you are creating?

8. Click Next. An Active Directory Domain Services Installation Wizard message box appears, warning you that your credentials might not be sufficient to create the new domain.

9. Click No, and then click Back to return to the *Network Credentials* page.

10. Select the Alternate credentials option, and then click Set. A Windows Security dialog box appears.

11. In the User name text box, key **Administrator**. In the Password text box, key **P@ssw0rd**, and click OK.

12. Click Next. The *Name the New Domain* page appears again with the domain name you specified still in place.

13. Click Next. The *Domain NetBIOS Name* page appears.

14. Click Next to accept the default value. The *Set Domain Functional Level* page appears.

15. In the Domain functional level drop-down list, select Windows Server 2008, and click Next. The *Select a Site* page appears.

16. Click Next to accept the default site name. The *Additional Domain Controller Options* page appears.

Question 2	Why is the Read-only domain controller (RODC) option grayed out on the Additional Domain Controller Options page?

17. Select the Global Catalog checkbox, and click Next. A Static IP Assignment message box appears, warning that the computer has dynamically assigned IP addresses.

18. Click Yes. The *Source Domain Controller* page appears.

19. Click Next to accept the default setting. The *Location for Database, Log Files, and SYSVOL* page appears.

20. Click Next to accept the default settings. The *Directory Services Restore Mode Administrator Password* page appears.

21. In the Password and Confirm Password text boxes, key **P@ssw0rd**, and click Next. The *Summary* page appears.

22. Click Next. The wizard installs Active Directory, and the *Completing the Active Directory Domain Services Installation Wizard* page appears.

23. Click Finish. An Active Directory Domain Services Installation Wizard message box appears, prompting you to restart the computer.

24. Click Restart Now. The computer restarts.

Exercise 3.3	Administering a Subdomain
Overview	You have been instructed to configure the new domain so that the administrators of the original contoso.com domain are able to manage it. In this exercise, you use group memberships to provide contoso.com users with access to the new subdomain.
Completion time	20 minutes

1. Log on to the new domain you created with the Domain##\Administrator account, where ## is the number assigned by your instructor, using the password *P@ssw0rd*.

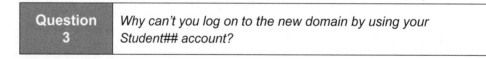

Question 3	Why can't you log on to the new domain by using your Student## account?

2. Press Ctrl+Prt Scr to take a screen shot of the Initial Configuration Tasks window, showing the new domain you created in Exercise 3.2, and then press Ctrl+V to paste the resulting image into the lab03_worksheet file in the page provided.

> **NOTE**   *If the Initial Configuration tasks window does not appear, open the Run dialog box, key **oobe** in the Open text box, and click OK.*

3. Click Start, and then click Administrative Tools > Active Directory Users and Computers. The Active Directory Users and Computers console appears, as shown in Figure 3-2.

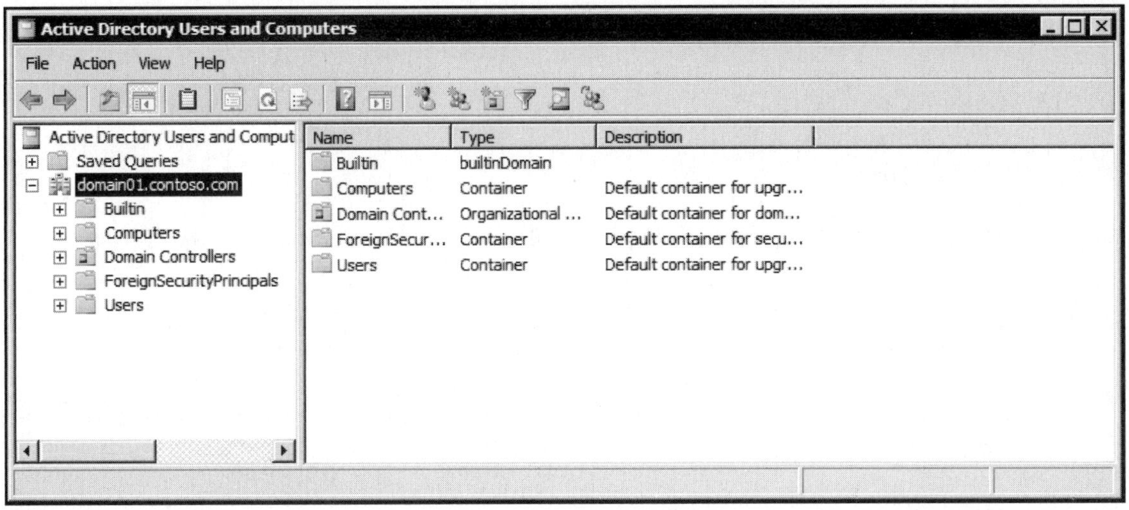

Figure 3-2
Active Directory Users and Computers console

4. Right-click the domain##.contoso.com domain and, from the context menu, select New > Organizational Unit. The New Object–Organizational Unit dialog box appears.

5. In the Name text box, key **Sales**, and click OK. The new organizational unit appears in the domain.

6. Right-click the Sales OU that you just created and, from the context menu, select New > User. The New Object–User Wizard appears.

7. In the First name text box, key **Mark**.

8. In the Last name text box, key **Lee**.

9. In the User logon name text box key **mlee** and click Next.

10. In the Password and Confirm password text boxes, key **P@ssw0rd**.

11. Clear the User must change password at next logon checkbox.

12. Select the Password never expires check box, and click Next.

13. Click Finish. The new user object appears in the Sales OU.

14. Right-click the domain##.contoso.com domain and, from the context menu, select Change Domain. The Change Domain dialog box appears.

15. In the Domain text box, key **contoso.com**, and click OK. The contoso.com domain appears in the console.

16. Right-click the contoso.com domain, and examine the context menu.

Question 4	Why are you unable to create new organizational unit or user objects in the contoso.com domain?

17. Open the Change Domain dialog box again, and change back to the domain##.contoso.com domain.

18. Expand the domain##.contoso.com domain, and select the Builtin container.

19. Right-click the Administrators group and, from the context menu, select Properties. The Administrators Properties sheet appears.

20. Click the Members tab, and then click Add. The Select Users, Contacts, Computers, Or Groups dialog box appears.

21. Click Locations. The Locations dialog box appears.

22. Select the contoso.com domain object, and click OK.

23. In the Enter the object names to select box, key **Students**, and click OK. The Students group appears in the Members list.

24. Click OK to close the Administrators Properties sheet.

Question 5	Are you now able to create new objects in the contoso.com domain? Why or why not?

25. Log off of the domain, and log on again by using your contoso.com\Student## account and the password *P@ssw0rd*.

26. Open the Active Directory Users and Computers console, and try to create a new user in the Sales OU by using the name Tracy Tallman and the password *P@ssw0rd*.

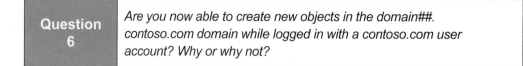

Question 6	Are you now able to create new objects in the domain##.contoso.com domain while logged in with a contoso.com user account? Why or why not?

27. Close the Active Directory Users And Groups console.

28. Log off of the computer.

Exercise 3.4   Removing a Domain

Overview	In this exercise, you remove the domain you created prior to creating a new forest.
Completion time	10 minutes

1. Log on to the contoso.com domain using the Administrator account and the password *P@ssw0rd*.

2. Open the Run dialog box, and open dcpromo.exe again. The Active Directory Domain Services Installation Wizard appears.

3. Click Next to bypass the Welcome page. An Active Directory Domain Services Installation Wizard message box appears, warning you that the computer is a global catalog server.

4. Click OK. The *Delete the Domain* page appears.

5. Select the Delete the domain because the server is the last domain controller in the domain checkbox, and click Next. The *Application Directory Partitions* page appears.

6. Click Next to continue. The *Confirm Deletion* page appears.

7. Select the Delete all application directory partitions on this Active Directory domain controller checkbox, and click Next. The *Network Credentials* page appears.

8. Click Next to accept the default settings. The *Remove DNS Delegation* page appears.

9. Click Next to accept the default Delete the DNS delegations pointing to this server setting.

10. The *Administrator Password* page appears.

11. In the Password and Confirm Password text boxes, key **P@ssw0rd**, and click Next. The *Summary* page appears.

12. Press Ctrl+Prt Scr to take a screen shot of the *Summary* page, and then press Ctrl+V to paste the resulting image into the lab03_worksheet file in the page provided.

13. Click Next to continue. The wizard removes the domain. The *Completing the Active Directory Domain Services Installation Wizard* page appears.

14. Click Finish. An Active Directory Domain Services Installation Wizard message box appears, prompting you to restart the computer.

15. Click Restart Now. The computer restarts.

Exercise 3.5	Creating a New Forest
Overview	Another possibility is to create a separate forest for the new division. In this exercise, you promote the domain controller again, this time keeping the new domain completely separate from the existing domain.
Completion time	15 minutes

1. Log on to the local machine as Administrator by using the password *P@ssw0rd*.

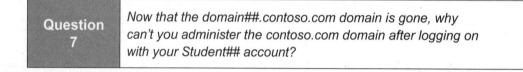

Question 7	Now that the domain##.contoso.com domain is gone, why can't you administer the contoso.com domain after logging on with your Student## account?

2. Press Ctrl+Prt Scr to take a screen shot of the Initial Configuration Tasks window, and then press Ctrl+V to paste the resulting image into the lab03_worksheet file in the page provided.

3. Open the Run dialog box, and open the dcpromo.exe program once again. The Active Directory Domain Services Installation Wizard appears.

4. Select the Use advanced mode installation checkbox, and click Next. The *Operating System Compatibility* page appears.

5. Click Next to continue. The *Choose a Deployment Configuration* page appears.

6. Select the Create *a new domain in a new forest* option, and then click Next. The *Name the Forest Root Domain* page appears.

7. In the FQDN of the forest root domain text box, key **domain##.com**, where ## is the number assigned to your computer by your instructor, and click Next. The *Domain NetBIOS Name* page appears.

8. Click Next to accept the default NetBIOS name. The *Set Forest Functional Level* page appears.

9. In the Forest functional level drop-down list, select Windows Server 2008, and click Next. The *Additional Domain Controller Options* page appears.

10. Click Next to accept the default settings. A Static IP Assignment message box appears, warning that the computer has dynamically assigned IP addresses.

11. Click Yes. An Active Directory Domain Services Installation Wizard message box appears, warning that the wizard cannot locate an authoritative zone for the domain.

12. Click Yes to continue. The *Location for Database, Log Files, and SYSVOL* page appears.

13. Click Next to accept the default settings. The *Directory Services Restore Mode Administrator Password* page appears.

14. In the Password and Confirm Password text boxes, key **P@ssw0rd**, and click Next. The *Summary* page appears.

15. Click Next. The wizard installs Active Directory, and the *Completing the Active Directory Domain Services Installation Wizard* page appears.

16. Click Finish. An Active Directory Domain Services Installation Wizard message box appears, prompting you to restart the computer.

17. Click Restart Now. The computer restarts.

Exercise 3.6	Administering Forests
Overview	In this exercise, you examine the administrative capabilities of the two forests in your Active Directory namespace.
Completion time	15 minutes

1. Log on to domain##.com with the Administrator account by using the password *P@ssw0rd*.

2. Click Start, and then click Administrative Tools > Active Directory Users and Computers. The Active Directory Users and Computers console appears.

3. Expand the domain##.com domain, as shown in Figure 3-3.

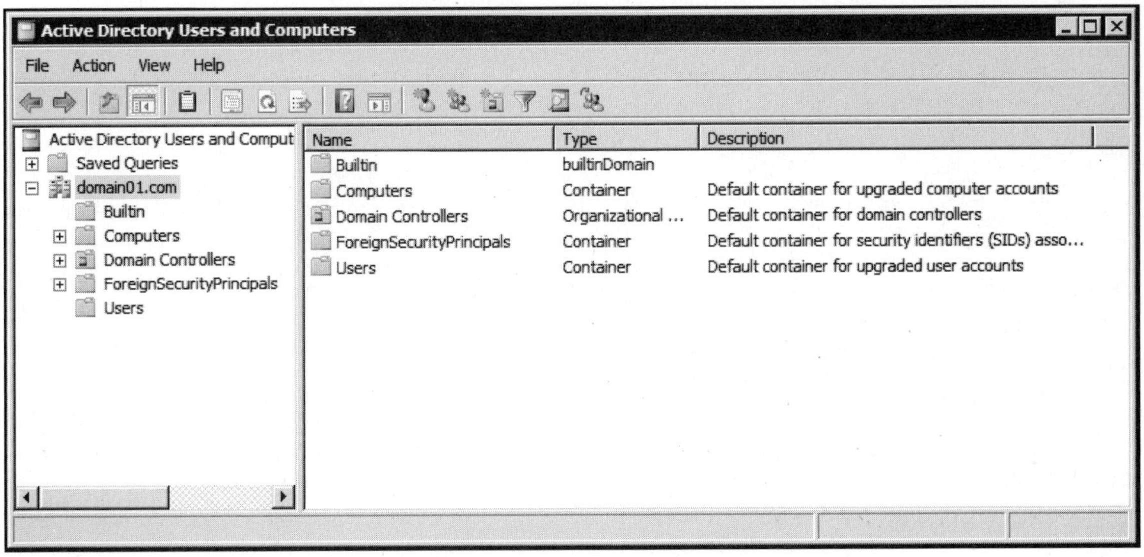

Figure 3-3
Domain##.com domain in the Active Directory Users and Computers console

4. In the domain, create a new organizational unit object named Sales and a new user object in the Sales OU with the name Mark Lee, the user logon name mlee, and the password *P@ssw0rd*.

Question 8	*What is the result?*

5. Right-click the domain##.com domain and, from the context menu, select Change Domain. The Change Domain dialog box appears.

6. In the Domain text box, key **contoso.com**, and click OK. A message box appears, indicating that the domain could not be found.

7. Click OK, and then click Cancel in the Change Domain dialog box.

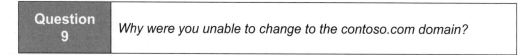

Question 9	*Why were you unable to change to the contoso.com domain?*

8. Select the Builtin container.

9. Right-click the Administrators group and, from the context menu, select Properties. The Administrators Properties sheet appears.

10. Click the Members tab, and then click Add. The Select Users, Contacts, Computers, Or Groups dialog box appears.

11. Click Locations. The Locations dialog box appears.

Question 10	*Why does the contoso.com domain not appear in the Locations dialog box?*

12. Press Ctrl+Prt Scr to take a screen shot of the Locations dialog box, and then press Ctrl+V to paste the resulting image into the lab03_worksheet file in the page provided.

13. Click Cancel three times to close the Locations dialog box; the Select Users, Contacts, Computers, or Groups dialog box; and the Administrators Properties sheet.

14. Close the Active Directory Users and Computers console.

15. Log off of the computer.

LAB REVIEW QUESTIONS

Completion time	10 minutes

1. In Exercise 3.2, if you selected the Create a new domain tree root checkbox instead of the Create a new child domain checkbox, how would the configuration of the contoso.com forest be different?

2. In Exercise 3.2, what was the difference between the Student## account you use to log on at the beginning of the lab and the domain Administrator account that enabled you to successfully create a new subdomain?

3. In Exercise 3.2, how many domain trees are in your Active Directory namespace after you create the new domain? How many forests?

4. In Exercise 3.5, how many domain trees are in your Active Directory namespace after you create the new domain (not counting the other student computers in the classroom)? How many forests?

LAB CHALLENGE: ADMINISTERING TWO FORESTS

Completion time	20 minutes

In Exercise 3.6, you were unable to administer the contoso.com domain while logged on to the new domain##.com forest you created. To complete this challenge, you must configure your computer so that you are able to create Active Directory objects in both domains using a single logon. List the steps you took to achieve this goal. Press Ctrl+Prt Scr to take a screen shot of the Active Directory Users And Computers console, showing the contoso.com domain, and then press Ctrl+V to paste the resulting image into the lab03_worksheet file in the page provided.

WORKSTATION RESET: RETURNING TO BASELINE

Completion time	20 minutes

To return the computer to its baseline state, complete the following procedures.

1. Repeat the procedure in Exercise 3.4 to remove the domain##.com domain.

2. Restart the computer.

3. Open the Server Manager console, and remove the Active Directory Domain Services and DNS Server roles that you installed during the course of the lab.

4. Restart the computer.

5. In the Initial Configuration Tasks window, click Configure Networking.

6. Right-click the Local Area Connection icon and, from the context menu, select Properties. The Local Area Connection Properties sheet appears.

7. Select the Internet Protocol Version 4 (TCP/IPv4) component, and click Properties. The Internet Protocol Version 4 (TCP/IPv4) Properties sheet appears.

8. Select the Obtain DNS server address automatically option, and click OK.

9. Click OK again to close the Local Area Connection Properties sheet.

10. In the Initial Configuration Tasks window, click Provide Computer Name and Domain. The System Properties sheet appears.

11. Click Change. The Computer Name/Domain Changes dialog box appears.

12. Click More. The DNS Suffix and NetBIOS Computer Name dialog box appears.

13. Clear the Primary DNS Suffix of this Computer text box, and click OK.

14. Select the Domain option. Key **contoso.com** in the text box, and then click Next. The Windows Security dialog box appears.

15. In the User Name text box, key **Student##**.

16. In the Password text box, key **P@ssw0rd**, and click OK. A Computer Name/Domain Changes message box appears, welcoming you to the domain.

17. Click OK twice.

18. Click Close to close the System Properties sheet and restart the computer.

LAB 4
DEPLOYING APPLICATIONS

This lab contains the following exercises and activities:

BEFORE YOU BEGIN

The classroom network consists of Windows Server 2008 student servers that are all connected to a local area network. There is also a classroom server, named ServerDC, that is

connected to the same classroom network. ServerDC is also running Windows Server 2008 and is the domain controller for a domain named contoso.com. Throughout the labs in this manual, you will be working with the same student server on which you will install, configure, maintain, and troubleshoot application roles, features, and services.

Your instructor should have supplied you with the information needed to fill in the following table:

Student computer name (Server##)	
Student account name (Student##)	

To complete the exercises in this lab, you will require access to a second student computer on the classroom network, referred to in the exercises as your *partner server*. Depending on the configuration of your network, use one of the following options as directed by your instructor:

- For a conventional classroom network with one operating system installed on each computer, you must have a lab partner with his or her own computer, performing the same exercises as yourself.

- For a classroom in which each computer uses local virtualization software to install multiple operating systems, you must run two virtual machines representing student computers and perform the exercises separately on each virtual machine.

- For a classroom that uses online virtualization, you will have access to two virtual student servers in your Web browser. You must perform the exercises separately on each virtual machine.

Working with Lab Worksheets

Each lab in this manual requires that you answer questions, shoot screen shots, or perform other activities that you are to document in a worksheet named for the lab, such as lab01_worksheet. Your instructor will supply you with the worksheet files by copying them to the Students\Worksheets share on ServerDC. As you perform the exercises in each lab, open the appropriate worksheet file using WordPad, fill in the required information, and save the file to your computer's Student##\Documents folder. This folder is automatically redirected to the ServerDC computer. Your instructor will examine these worksheet files to assess your performance.

The procedure for opening and saving a worksheet file is as follows:

1. Click Start, and then click Run. The Run dialog box appears.

2. In the Open text box, key **\\ServerDC\Students\Worksheets\lab##_worksheet** (where lab## contains the number of the lab you're completing), and click OK.

3. The worksheet document opens in Wordpad.

4. Complete all of the exercises in the worksheet.

5. In WordPad, choose Save As from the File menu. The Save As dialog box appears.

6. In the File Name text box, key **lab##_worksheet_*yourname*** (where lab## contains the number of the lab you're completing and *yourname* is your last name), and click Save.

SCENARIO

You are an administrator for Contoso, Ltd., assigned to the test lab. Your supervisor wants to investigate various methods of deploying applications on network computers other than performing individual, manual installation. Toward this end, you begin exploring the capabilities of the Terminal Services role included with Windows Server 2008.

After completing this lab, you will be able to:

■ Install the Terminal Services role

■ Configure the Remote Desktop Connection client

■ Deploy RemoteApp applications

Estimated lab time: 130 minutes

Exercise 4.1	Installing the Terminal Services Role
Overview	For Windows Server 2008 to function as a terminal server, you must first install the Terminal Services role. In this exercise, you add the role with the Terminal Server role service, enabling the server to provide basic Terminal Services functionality.
Completion time	10 minutes

1. Turn on your computer. When the logon screen appears, log on using your Student## account and the password *P@ssw0rd*.

2. Close the Initial Configuration Tasks window when it appears.

3. Click Start, point to Administrative Tools, and click Server Manager. Click Continue in the User Account Control message box, and the Server Manager console appears.

4. Select the Roles node, and click Add Roles. The Add Roles Wizard appears, displaying the *Before You Begin* page.

5. Click Next to continue. The *Select Server Roles* page appears.

> **NOTE**
> *If your computer already has other roles or features installed, remove them before you proceed with this lab.*

6. Select the Terminal Services role, and click Next. The *Introduction to Terminal Services* page appears.

7. Click Next to bypass the introductory page. The *Select Role Services* page appears, as shown in Figure 4-1.

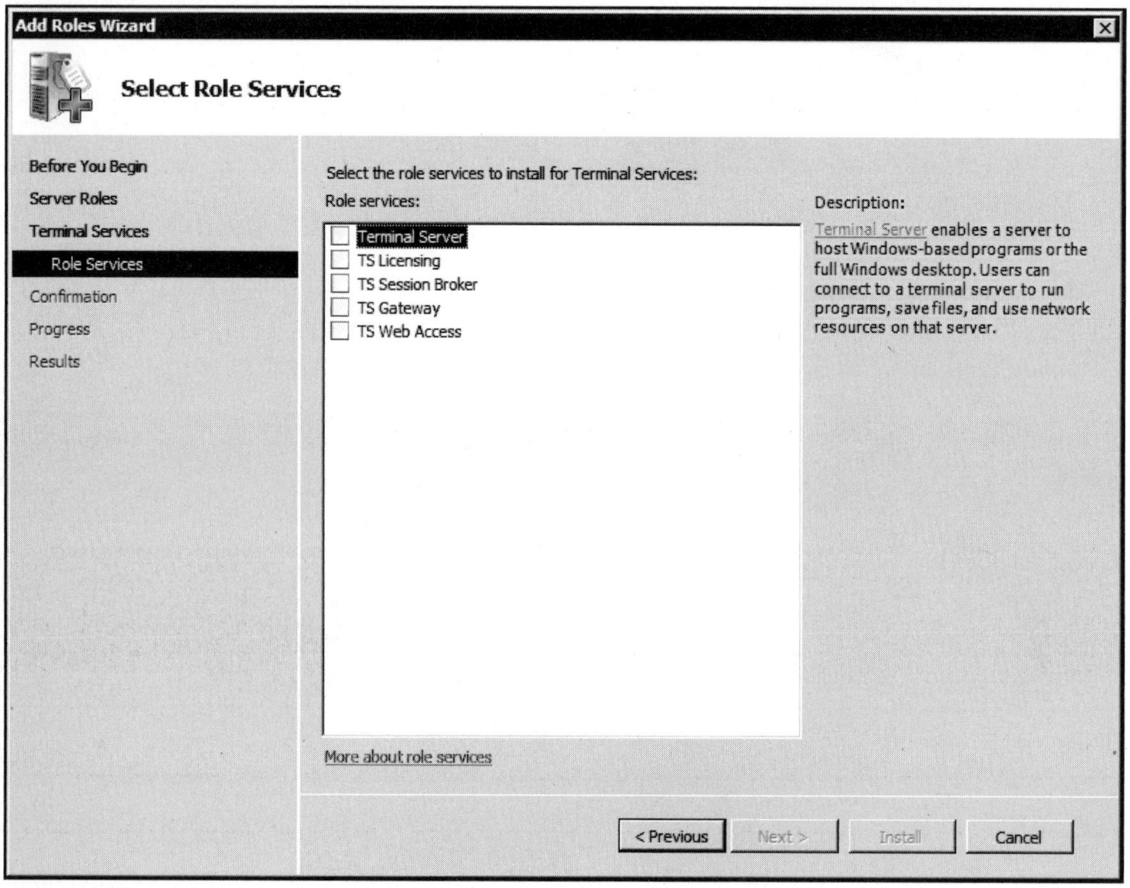

Figure 4-1
Select Role Services page of the Add Roles Wizard

8. Select the Terminal Server role service, and click Next. The *Uninstall and Reinstall Applications for Compatibility* page appears.

9. Click Next to continue. The *Specify Authentication Method for Terminal Server* page appears.

10. Select the Do not require Network Level Authentication option, and click Next. The *Specify Licensing Mode* page appears.

11. Select the Configure Later option, and click Next. The *Select User Groups Allowed Access To This Terminal Server* page appears.

12. Click Add. The Select Users, Computers, or Groups dialog box appears.

13. In the Enter Object Names to Select box, key **Students**, and click OK.

14. Press Ctrl+Prt Scr to take a screen shot of the *Select User Groups Allowed Access To This Terminal Server* page, and then press Ctrl+V to paste the resulting image into the lab04_worksheet file in the page provided.

15. Click Next to accept the specified groups. The *Confirm Installation Selections* page appears.

16. Click Install. The wizard installs the role, and the *Installation Results* page appears.

17. Click Close. An Add Roles Wizard message box appears, prompting you to restart the computer.

18. Click Yes. The computer restarts.

19. When the logon screen appears, log on using your Student## account and the password *P@ssw0rd.* Server Manager loads and completes the role installation.

20. Click Close to close the Resume Configuration Wizard.

21. Close Server Manager, and leave the computer logged on for the next exercise.

Exercise 4.2	Configuring the Remote Desktop Connection Client
Overview	In this exercise, you configure the Remote Desktop Connection client, preparing it to connect to a terminal server.
Completion time	10 minutes

1. Click Start, and then click All Programs > Accessories > Notepad. A Notepad window appears.

2. Key some text in the Notepad window, and then click File > Save As. The Save As combo box appears.

3. Save the text file to your Documents folder, using the name **Lab04**.

4. Close the Notepad window.

5. Click Start, and then click All Programs > Accessories > Remote Desktop Connection. The Remote Desktop Connection dialog box appears.

6. Click Options. The dialog box expands, as shown in Figure 4-2.

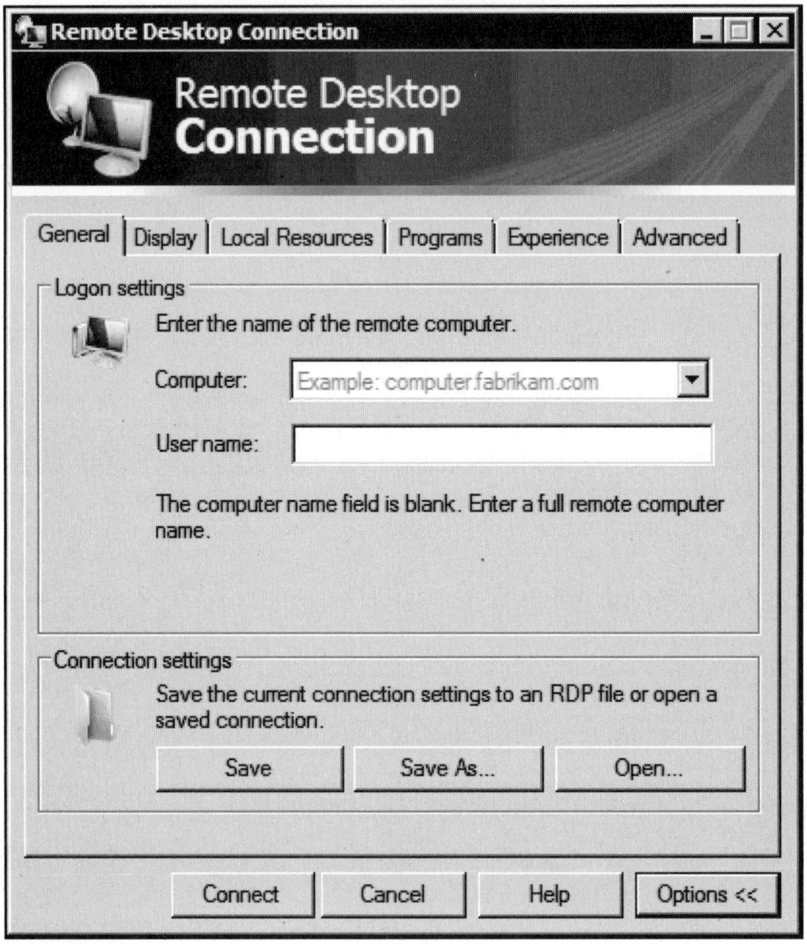

Figure 4-2
Remote Desktop Connection dialog box

7. Click the Display tab.

8. In the Remote Desktop Size box, use the slider to select a resolution just below that of your current display.

9. Click the Local Resources tab.

10. In the Remote Computer Sound box, select Do Not Play from the drop-down list.

11. In the Local Devices and Resources box, clear the Printers checkbox, and leave the Clipboard checkbox selected.

12. Click the Experience tab.

13. In the Performance drop-down list, select LAN (10 Mbps Or Higher).

14. Click the General tab.

15. Leave the Remote Desktop Connection window open for the next exercise.

Exercise 4.3	Establishing a Terminal Services Connection
Overview	In this exercise, you use the Remote Desktop Connection client to initiate a Terminal Services connection to your partner server.
Completion time	10 minutes

NOTE	*Before you initiate the connection to your partner server, make sure that Exercise 4.1 has been completed on that computer and that it is ready to receive remote connections.*

1. In the Remote Desktop Connection client program, on the General tab, key **Server##** in the Computer text box, where ## is the number assigned to your partner server by your instructor.

2. In the User Name field, key **contoso\student##**, where ## is the number assigned to your computer.

3. Click Connect. A Windows Security dialog box appears.

4. Under the contoso\student## user name, key **P@ssw0rd**, and click OK. A Server## - Remote Desktop window appears, containing the Initial Configuration Tasks window.

5. Close the Initial Configuration Tasks window.

6. In the Server## - Remote Desktop window, click Start, and then click All Programs > Accessories > Notepad. A Notepad window appears.

Question 1	*On which computer is the Notepad application actually running?*

7. Click File > Open. The Open combo box appears.

8. Press Ctrl+Prt Scr to take a screen shot of the Server## - Remote Desktop window, showing the Open combo box, and then press Ctrl+V to paste the resulting image into the lab04_worksheet file in the page provided.

Question 2	On which computer is the user profile stored that appears within the Student## folder (where ## is the number assigned to your computer)?

9. Select the Lab04 text file you created at the beginning of this exercise, and click Open.

10. Modify the text in the file, and save it.

11. Leave the Notepad window open, and click the Close button in the title bar of the Server## - Remote Desktop window. A Disconnect Terminal Services Session message box appears, asking whether you want to disconnect.

12. Click OK. The RDC client disconnects from the terminal server.

Question 3	Is Notepad still running on your partner server? Explain why or why not.

13. Leave the computer logged on for the next exercise.

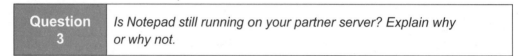

Exercise 4.4	Creating an RDP File
Overview	In this exercise, you use the RDC client to create an RDP file, which you can use to connect to a specific terminal server using a predetermined collection of configuration settings.
Completion time	10 minutes

1. Click Start, and then click All Programs > Accessories > Remote Desktop Connection. The Remote Desktop Connection dialog box appears.

2. Click Options. The dialog box expands.

3. In the Connection Settings box, click Save As. The Save As combo box appears.

4. Click Browse Folders. The combo box expands, as shown in Figure 4-3.

5. In the left pane, click Desktop.

6. In the File Name text box, key **Server##**, where ## is the number assigned to your partner server.

7. Click Save. A Server## icon appears on your desktop.

8. Click the Display tab.

9. In the Remote Desktop Size box, set the slider to Full Screen.

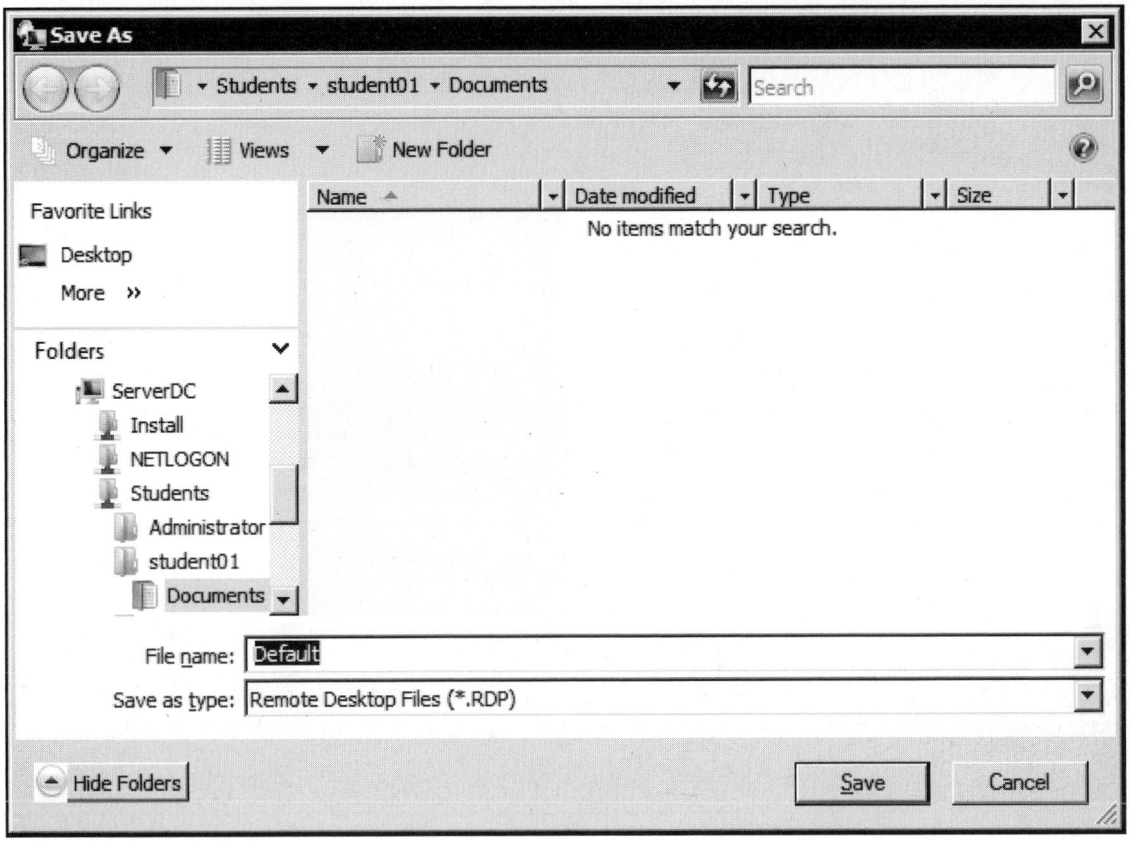

Figure 4-3
Save As combo box

10. Click Connect. A Remote Desktop Connection message box appears, asking whether you trust the remote connection.

11. Click Connect. The Windows Security dialog box appears.

12. Log on using the password *P@ssw0rd*, and click OK. The RDC client connects to the terminal server and the desktop appears, with the Notepad window you opened in Exercise 4.2 still open.

Question 4	*Is the taskbar at the bottom of your screen being generated by your server or your partner server? How can you tell?*

13. Click the Close button in the connection bar to disconnect from the terminal server session.

14. Press Ctrl+Prt Scr to take a screen shot of your server's desktop, showing the Server## RDP icon, and then press Ctrl+V to paste the resulting image into the lab04_worksheet file in the page provided.

15. Double-click the Server## icon. A Remote Desktop Connection message box appears, warning you that the publisher of the remote connection cannot be identified.

16. Click Connect, log on using the password *P@ssw0rd*, and click OK. The RDC client connects to the terminal server.

17. In the remote session window, click Start. Click the arrow button and, on the context menu, click Log Off.

Question 5	What happens?

Question 6	Is the Notepad application you opened in Exercise 4.2 still open in the terminal server session? Why or why not?

18. Leave the computer logged on for the next exercise.

Exercise 4.5	Configuring RemoteApp Applications
Overview	In this exercise, you configure your terminal server to deploy individual applications using RemoteApp.
Completion time	10 minutes

1. Click Start, and then click Administrative Tools > Terminal Services > TS RemoteApp Manager. Click Continue in the User Account Control message box, and the TS RemoteApp Manager console appears, as shown in Figure 4-4.

2. In the actions pane, click Add RemoteApp Programs. The RemoteApp Wizard appears.

3. Click Next to bypass the Welcome page. The *Choose Programs To Add To The RemoteApp Programs List* page appears.

4. Select the WordPad checkbox, and click Properties. The RemoteApp Properties sheet for WordPad appears.

5. Clear the RemoteApp program is available through TS Web Access checkbox.

6. Select the Allow any command line arguments option, and click OK. A RemoteApp Wizard message box appears, warning you that allowing executable files to run with no restrictions on the command line arguments opens the terminal server to attack.

7. Click Yes.

8. Click Next. The *Review Settings* page appears.

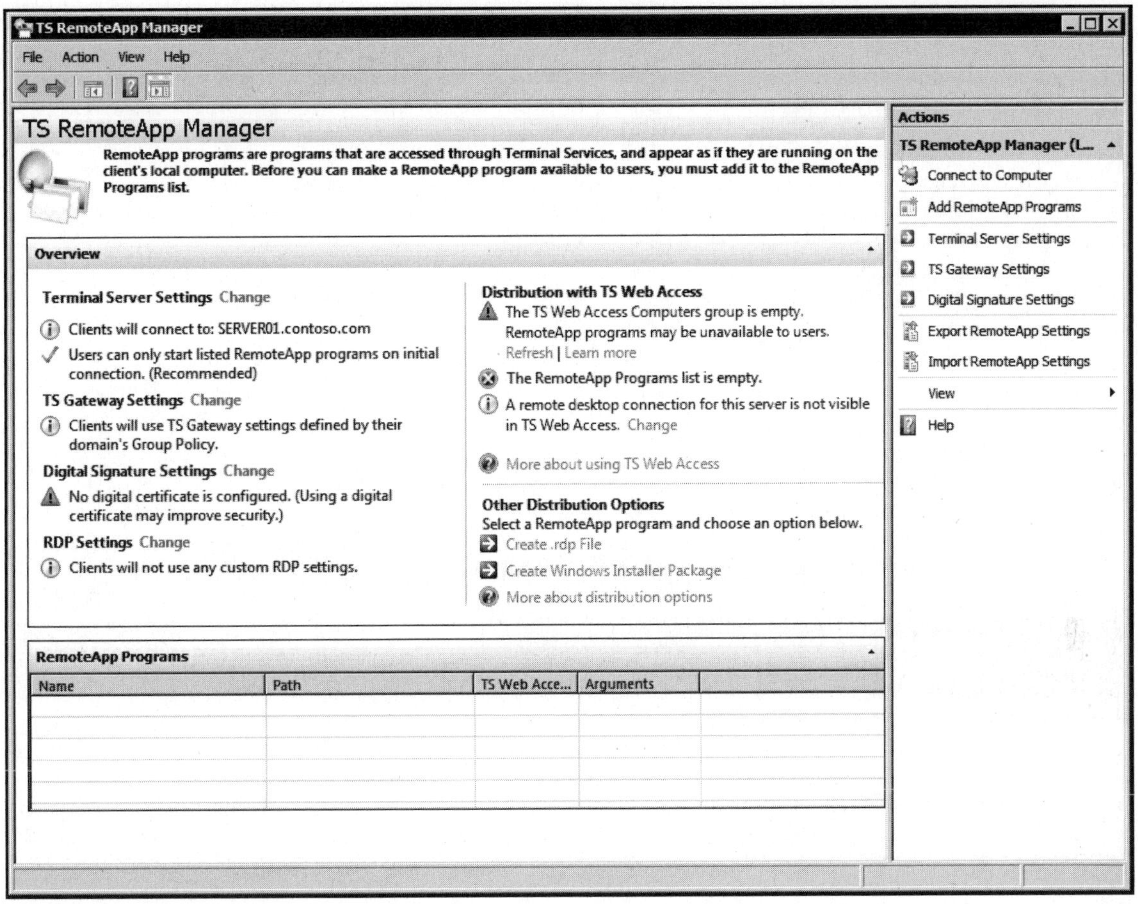

Figure 4-4
TS RemoteApp Manager console

9. Click Finish. The WordPad application appears in the RemoteApp Programs list.

10. Repeat steps 2 to 9 to add the Server Manager and System Information applications to the RemoteApp Programs list, clearing the RemoteApp program is available through TS Web Access checkbox and leaving the default Do not allow command line arguments setting for each.

11. Press Ctrl+Prt Scr to take a screen shot of the TS RemoteApp Manager console, showing the applications you added, and then press Ctrl+V to paste the resulting image into the lab04_worksheet file in the page provided.

> | **Question 7** | *In the TS RemoteApp Manager console, there are currently two warning indicators showing in the Overview area. Will any of these warnings make it impossible to access your RemoteApp applications from your partner server? Explain why or why not.* |
> | --- | --- |

12. Leave the TS RemoteApp Manager console open for the next exercise.

Exercise 4.6	Creating RemoteApp RDP Files
Overview	In this exercise, you create RDP files that enable clients to access the RemoteApp applications you configured in Exercise 4.5.
Completion time	10 minutes

1. In the TS RemoteApp Manager console, in the RemoteApp Programs list, select the WordPad application you added in Exercise 4.5.

2. In the actions pane, select Create .rdp File. The RemoteApp Wizard appears.

3. Click Next to bypass the *Welcome to the RemoteApp Wizard* page. The *Specify Package Settings* page appears, as shown in Figure 4-5.

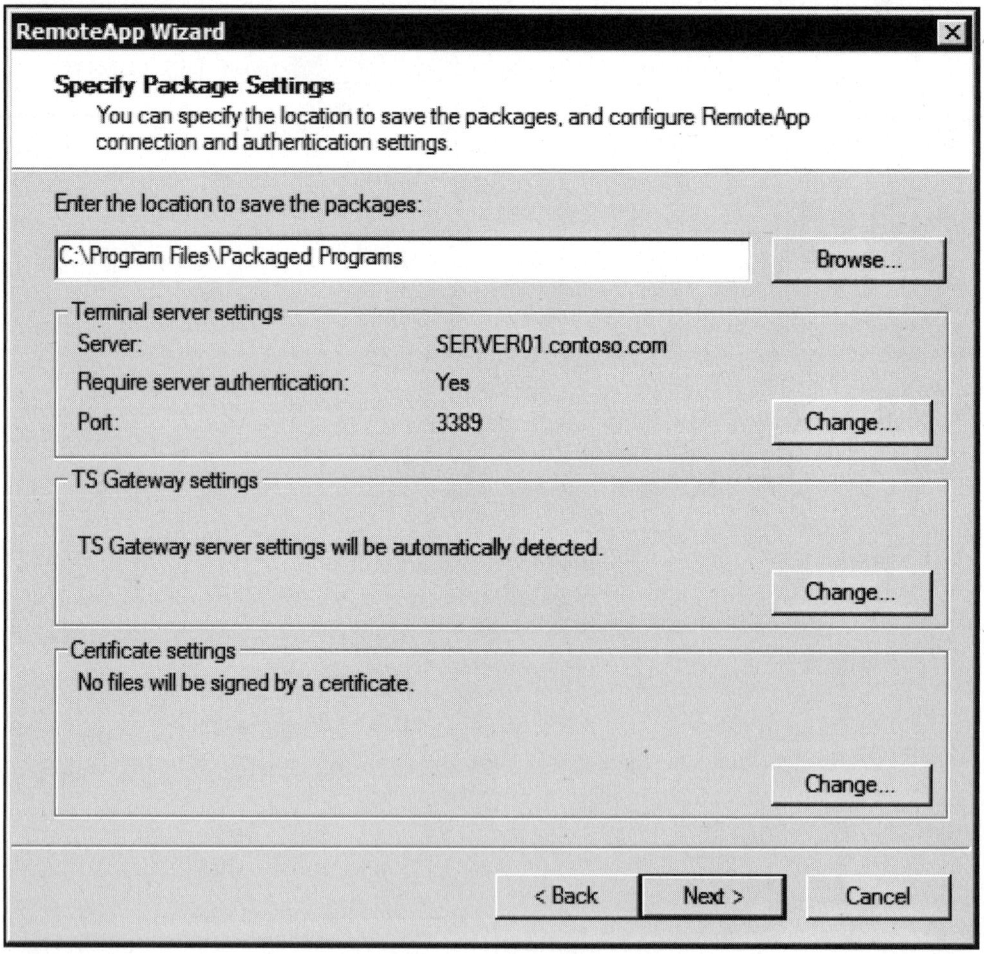

Figure 4-5
Specify Package Settings page of the RemoteApp Wizard

4. In the Enter the location to save the packages text box, key **serverdc\students\ student##\documents**, where ## is the number assigned to your computer, and then click Next. The *Review Settings* page appears.

5. Click Finish. The wizard closes, and an RDP file named for the application appears in your Documents folder.

6. Repeat steps 2 to 5 to create an RDP file for the System Information application in your Documents folder.

7. Close the TS RemoteApp Manager console.

8. Log off of the computer.

Exercise 4.7	Launching RemoteApp RDP Files
Overview	In this exercise, you use the RDP files you created in Exercise 4.6 to establish terminal server connections from your partner server.
Completion time	10 minutes

1. Move to your partner server, and log on to the domain using your Student## account, where ## is the number assigned to your computer, and the password *P@ssw0rd*.

2. Click Start, and then click All Programs > Accessories > Windows Explorer. A Windows Explorer window appears, displaying the contents of your Documents folder.

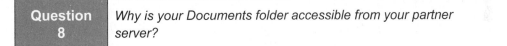

Question 8	Why is your Documents folder accessible from your partner server?

3. In the Documents folder, double-click the WordPad RDP file. A RemoteApp message box appears, warning that the publisher of the remote connection cannot be identified.

4. Click Connect. A Windows Security dialog box appears.

5. Log on using your contoso\Student## account and the password *P@ssw0rd*. A WordPad window appears.

Question 9	On which computer is the Wordpad.exe file running?

6. In the WordPad window, click File > Open. The Open combo box appears.

7. Browse to the Local Disk (C:) drive.

Question 10	Are you looking at the Local Disk (C:) drive on your partner server or on your computer, the terminal server? How can you tell?

8. Click Cancel to close the Open combo box.

9. While still on your partner server, switch back to Windows Explorer, and double-click the Msinfo32 RDP file for the System Information application.

10. Click Connect to bypass the Unknown Publisher warning. The System Information window appears.

Question 11	For which computer does the System Information window contain information?

11. Close the Wordpad and System Information windows.

12. Log off of your partner computer.

Exercise 4.8	Creating Windows Installer Files
Overview	In this exercise, you create Windows Installer (.msi) package files that you can use to deploy your RemoteApp applications all over the network.
Completion time	10 minutes

1. Return to your own computer, and log on using your Student## account and the password *P@ssw0rd*.

2. Close the Initial Configuration Tasks window when it appears.

3. Open the TS RemoteApp Manager console and, in the RemoteApp Programs list, select the Server Manager application you added in Exercise 4.5.

4. In the actions pane, select Create Windows Installer Package. The RemoteApp Wizard appears.

5. Click Next to bypass the *Welcome to the RemoteApp Wizard* page. The *Specify Package Settings* page appears.

6. In the Enter the location to save the packages text box, key **serverdc\students\ student##\documents**, where ## is the number assigned to your computer, and then click Next. The *Configure Distribution Package* page appears, as shown in Figure 4-6.

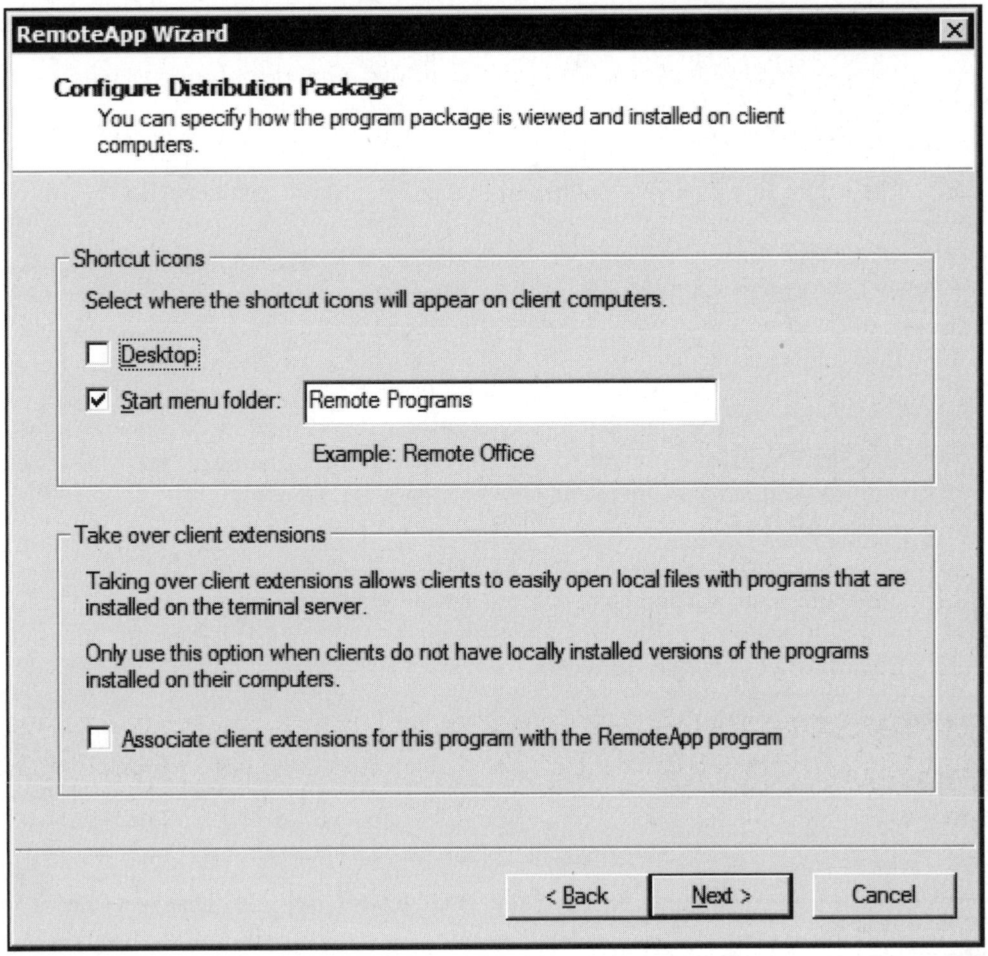

Figure 4-6
Configure Distribution Package page of the RemoteApp Wizard

7. In the Start menu folder text box, key **Server## Remote Programs**, where ## is the number assigned to your computer, and then click Next. The *Review Settings* page appears.

8. Click Finish. The wizard closes, and a Windows Installer file with the name CompMgmtLauncher appears in your Documents folder.

9. Close the TS RemoteApp Manager console.

10. Log off of the computer.

Exercise 4.9	Running Windows Installer Files
Overview	In this exercise, you move to your partner server and launch the Windows Installer package file you created in Exercise 4.8.
Completion time	10 minutes

1. Move to your partner server, and log on using your Student## account, where ## is the number assigned to your computer, and the password *P@ssw0rd*.

2. Open Windows Explorer. The contents of your Documents folder appear.

3. In the Documents folder, double-click the CompMgmtLauncher file.

4. If a Open File – Security Warning dialog box appears, click Run. A User Account Control dialog box appears.

5. Click Allow.

6. While still on your partner server, click Start, and then click All Programs > Server## Remote Programs > Server Manager. A RemoteApp message box appears, warning that the publisher of the remote connection cannot be identified.

7. Click Connect. A Windows Security dialog box appears.

8. Log on using your contoso\Student## account with the password *P@ssw0rd*. A Connected To Server##.contoso.com window appears, containing another User Account Control dialog box.

9. Press Ctrl+Prt Scr to take a screen shot of the Connected to SERVER##.contoso.com window, and then press Ctrl+V to paste the resulting image into the lab04_worksheet file in the page provided.

10. In the User Account Control dialog box, click Continue. The Server Manager console appears.

Question 12	Why did two User Account Control dialog boxes appear during the terminal server connection sequence?

11. Close the Server Manager console.

12. Log off of the computer.

LAB REVIEW QUESTIONS

Completion time	10 minutes

1. In Exercise 4.2, you created a Lab04 text file on your computer at the beginning of the exercise. Later, while working within a terminal server session on your partner server, you opened a file using Notepad and accessed the Documents folder in your user profile on that computer. Why does the Lab04 file appear in the Documents folder on your partner server when you originally created it on your own server?

2. In Exercises 4.4 and 4.7, you used the RDC client to connect to your partner server on two separate occasions, once interactively and once using the RDP file you created. How can you tell from this experience that the RDP file includes the settings you configured in the client before you created the RDP file?

3. In Exercise 4.7, you opened two separate RemoteApp applications on your computer using your partner server as the client. How many sessions did you open on the terminal server by launching these two applications? How can you tell?

LAB CHALLENGE: DEPLOYING REMOTEAPP APPLICATIONS USING GROUP POLICY

Completion time	20 minutes

Your supervisor wants to be able to deploy terminal server applications to users' desktops using RemoteApp and Group Policy, without the need for any configuration by the user. To complete this challenge, demonstrate that this is possible by deploying the Calculator program on your terminal server to all other computers in the classroom. As you proceed, be sure to observe the following restrictions.

-   Make sure your deployed application is properly identified on the users' desktops as Server## Calculator, where ## is the number assigned to your computer.

-   Do not modify any of the existing Group Policy objects in the Active Directory tree. Create your own GPO, naming it Student##, and link it as needed.

On your worksheet, list all of the tasks you must perform to complete this challenge.

WORKSTATION RESET: RETURNING TO BASELINE

Completion time	10 minutes

To return the computer to its baseline state, complete the following procedures.

1. Open the Group Policy Management console, and unlink any GPOs you created during the course of the lab.

2. Open the Server Manager console, and remove the Terminal Services role.

LAB 5
USING FILE AND PRINT SERVICES

This lab contains the following exercises and activities:

BEFORE YOU BEGIN

The classroom network consists of Windows Server 2008 student servers that are all connected to a local area network. There is also a classroom server, named ServerDC, that is

connected to the same classroom network. ServerDC is also running Windows Server 2008 and is the domain controller for a domain named contoso.com. Throughout the labs in this manual, you will be working with the same student server on which you will install, configure, maintain, and troubleshoot application roles, features, and services.

Your instructor should have supplied you with the information needed to fill in the following table:

Student computer name (Server##)	
Student account name (Student##)	

To complete the exercises in this lab, you will require access to a second student computer on the classroom network, referred to in the exercises as your *partner server*. Depending on the configuration of your network, use one of the following options as directed by your instructor:

- For a conventional classroom network with one operating system installed on each computer, you must have a lab partner with his or her own computer, performing the same exercises as yourself.

- For a classroom in which each computer uses local virtualization software to install multiple operating systems, you must run two virtual machines representing student computers and perform the exercises separately on each virtual machine.

- For a classroom that uses online virtualization, you will have access to two virtual student servers in your Web browser. You must perform the exercises separately on each virtual machine.

Working with Lab Worksheets

Each lab in this manual requires that you answer questions, shoot screen shots, or perform other activities that you are to document in a worksheet named for the lab, such as lab01_worksheet. Your instructor will supply you with the worksheet files by copying them to the Students\Worksheets share on ServerDC. As you perform the exercises in each lab, open the appropriate worksheet file using WordPad, fill in the required information, and save the file to your computer's Student##\Documents folder. This folder is automatically redirected to the ServerDC computer. Your instructor will examine these worksheet files to assess your performance.

The procedure for opening and saving a worksheet file is as follows:

1. Click Start, and then click Run. The Run dialog box appears.

2. In the Open text box, key **\\ServerDC\Students\Worksheets\lab##_worksheet** (where lab## contains the number of the lab you're completing), and click OK.

3. The worksheet document opens in Wordpad.

4. Complete all of the exercises in the worksheet.

5. In WordPad, choose Save As from the File menu. The Save As dialog box appears.

6. In the File Name text box, key **lab##_worksheet_*yourname*** (where lab## contains the number of the lab you're completing and *yourname* is your last name), and click Save.

SCENARIO

You are an administrator for Contoso, Ltd., assigned to the test lab. Your supervisor has instructed you to demonstrate the capabilities of the file and print services included with Windows Server 2008.

After completing this lab, you will be able to:

■ Install the File Services and Print Services roles

■ Create and manage a DFS namespace

■ Install a printer

■ Deploy printers in Active Directory

Estimated lab time: 130 minutes

Exercise 5.1	Installing the File and Print Services Roles
Overview	In this exercise, you prepare your lab server for the demonstration by installing the roles that implement advanced file and print tools in Windows Server 2008.
Completion time	10 minutes

1. Turn on your computer. When the logon screen appears, log on using your Student## account and the password *P@ssw0rd*.

2. Close the Initial Configuration Tasks window when it appears.

3. Click Start, point to Administrative Tools, and click Server Manager. Click Continue in the User Account Control message box, and the Server Manager console appears.

4. Select the Roles node, and click Add Roles. The Add Roles Wizard appears, displaying the *Before You Begin* page.

5. Click Next to continue. The *Select Server Roles* page appears.

If your computer already has other roles installed, remove them before you proceed with this lab.

6. Select the File Services and Print Services checkboxes, and click Next. The *Introduction to Print Services* page appears.

7. Click Next to bypass the introductory page. The *Select Role Services* page appears, as shown in Figure 5-1.

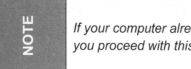

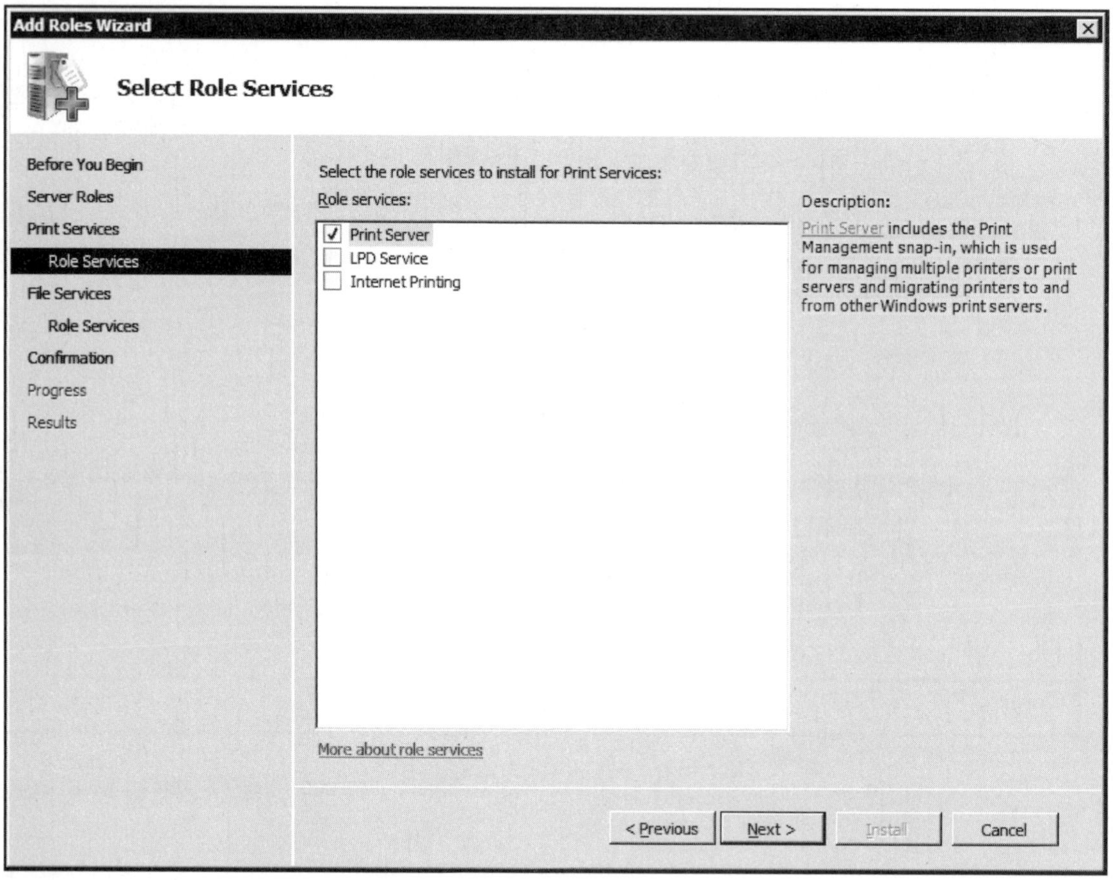

Add Roles Wizard ✕

Select Role Services

Before You Begin
Server Roles
Print Services
   Role Services
File Services
   Role Services
Confirmation
Progress
Results

Select the role services to install for Print Services:

Role services:

- ☑ Print Server
- ☐ LPD Service
- ☐ Internet Printing

Description:

Print Server includes the Print Management snap-in, which is used for managing multiple printers or print servers and migrating printers to and from other Windows print servers.

More about role services

< Previous   Next >   Install   Cancel

Figure 5-1
Select Role Services page for the Print Services role

8. Click Next to accept the default Print Server role service. The *Introduction to File Services* page appears.

9. Click Next to bypass the introductory page. The *Select Role Services* page appears, as shown in Figure 5-2.

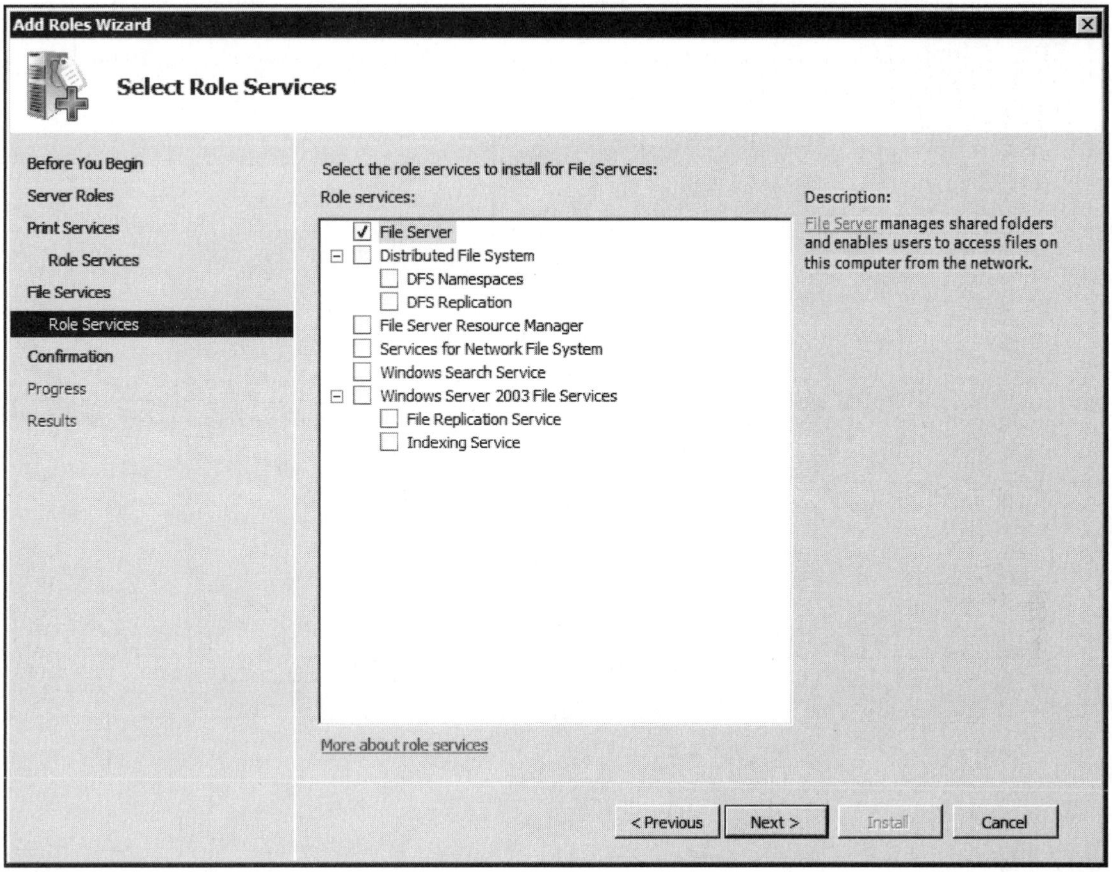

Figure 5-2
Select Role Services page for the File Services role

10. Select the Distributed File System role service, and click Next. The *Create a DFS Namespace* page appears.

11. Select the Create a namespace later using the DFS Management snap-in in Server Manager option, and click Next. The *Confirm Installation Selections* page appears.

12. Click Install. The wizard installs the roles, and the *Installation Results* page appears.

13. Click Close.

14. Close the Server Manager console, and leave the computer logged on for the next exercise.

Exercise 5.2	Creating a Volume Using Share and Storage Management
Overview	In this exercise you demonstrate the ability to provision storage in the new Share and Storage Management console in Windows Server 2008.
Completion time	10 minutes

1. Click Start, and then click Administrative Tools > Share and Storage Management. After you click Continue in the User Account Control message box, the Share and Storage Management console appears, as shown in Figure 5-3.

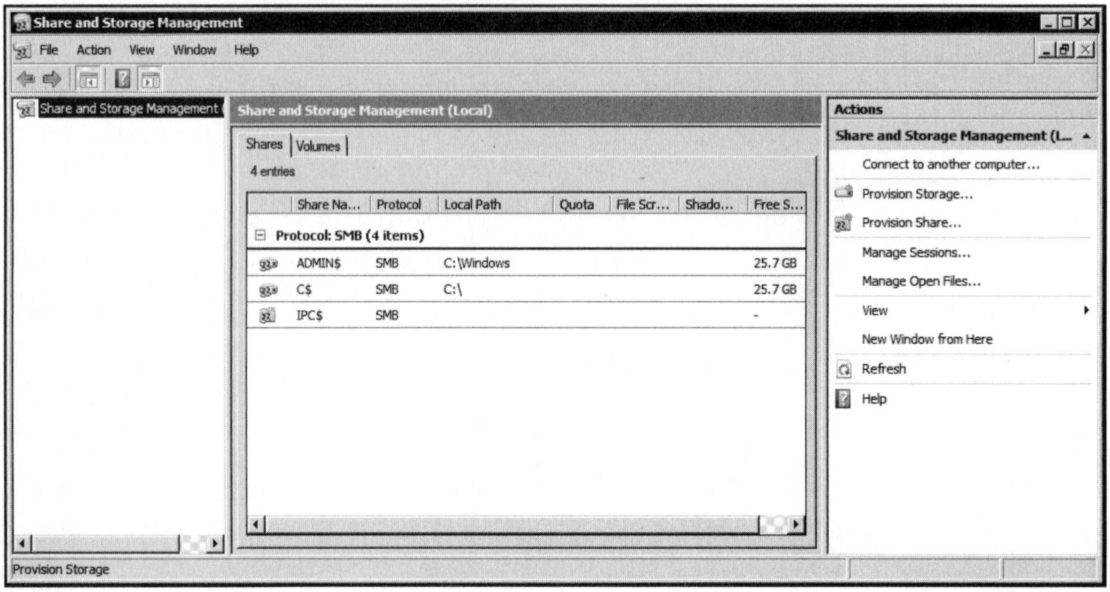

Figure 5-3
Share and Storage Management console

2. In the actions pane, click Provision Storage. The Provision Storage Wizard appears, displaying the *Storage Source* page.

3. Click Next to accept the default One or more disks available on this server option. The *Disk Drive* page appears.

4. Select Disk 1, and click Next. The *Volume Size* page appears.

> **NOTE**
> *If Disk 1 does not appear in the Provision Storage Wizard, open the Computer Management console, select the Disk Management snap-in, and make sure that Disk 1 is initialized.*

5. In the Specify a size for the new volume spin box, select a value that represents half the total size of Disk 1, and then click Next. The *Volume Creation* page appears.

6. Leave the Assign drive letter to this volume option selected. From the drop-down list, select the drive letter X, and then click Next. The *Format* page appears.

7. Leave the Format volume checkbox selected and, in the Volume label text box, key **Docs**. Leave the other settings at their defaults, and click Next. The *Review Settings And Create Storage* page appears.

8.   Click Create. The wizard creates and formats the volume.

9.   Click Close.

10. Press Ctrl+Prt Scr to take a screen shot of the Volumes tab in the Share and Storage Management console, showing the volume you just created, and then press Ctrl+V to paste the resulting image into the lab05_worksheet file in the page provided.

11. Leave the Sharing and Storage Management console open for the next exercise.

Exercise 5.3	Creating a Share Using Share and Storage Management
Overview	In this exercise, you demonstrate the ability to create and manage shares in the Share and Storage Management console in Windows Server 2008.
Completion time	10 minutes

1.   In the Sharing and Storage Management console, click Provision Share. The Provision A Shared Folder Wizard appears, displaying the *Shared Folder Location* page.

2.   Click Browse. The Browse For Folder dialog box appears.

3.   Select the x$ share, and click Make New Folder. Key **Docs**, and click OK. The x:\Docs path appears in the Location text box.

4.   Click Next. The *NTFS Permissions* page appears.

5.   Select the Yes, change NTFS permissions option, and click Edit Permissions. The Permissions for Docs dialog box appears.

> **NOTE** *The share administration policies in your company call for all access control to be performed using NTFS permissions, not share permissions.*

6.   Click Add. The Select Users, Computers, or Groups dialog box appears.

7.   In the Enter the object names to select box, key **Students; Domain Admins**, and click OK. The two security principals appear in the Group or user names list.

8.   Select the Domain Admins group. In the Permissions for Domain Admins box, select the Allow Full Control checkbox, and then click Apply.

9.   Select the Students group. In the Permissions for Students box, select the Allow Write and Allow Modify checkboxes, and then click Apply.

10. Press Ctrl+Prt Scr to take a screen shot of the Permissions for Docs dialog box, showing the NTFS permissions assigned to the Students group, and then press Ctrl+V to paste the resulting image into the lab05_worksheet file in the page provided.

11. Click OK to close the Permissions for Docs dialog box.

12. Click Next. The *Share Protocols* page appears.

13. Leave the SMB checkbox selected. In the Share Name text box, key **Documents**, and then click Next. The *SMB Settings* page appears.

14. Click Advanced. The Advanced dialog box appears.

15. Select the Enable access-based enumeration checkbox, and click OK.

16. Click Next. The *SMB Permissions* page appears.

17. Select the Users and groups have custom share permissions option, and click Permissions. The Permissions for Documents dialog box appears.

18. Select Everyone. In the Permissions for Everyone box, select Allow Full Control, and then click OK.

19. Click Next. The *DFS Namespace Publishing* page appears.

20. Click Next. The *Review Settings And Create Share* page appears.

21. Click Create. The wizard creates the share.

22. Click Close.

23. Press Ctrl+Prt Scr to take a screen shot of the Share and Storage Management console, showing the share you just created, and then press Ctrl+V to paste the resulting image into the lab05_worksheet file in the page provided.

24. Close the Share and Storage Management console.

25. Leave the computer logged on for the next exercise.

Exercise 5.4	Creating a DFS Namespace
Overview	In this exercise, you use the Distributed File System role service to create a DFS namespace that takes advantage of Active Directory Domain Services.
Completion time	10 minutes

1. Click Start, and then click Administrative Tools > DFS Management. Click Continue in the User Account Control message box, and the DFS Management console appears, as shown in Figure 5-4.

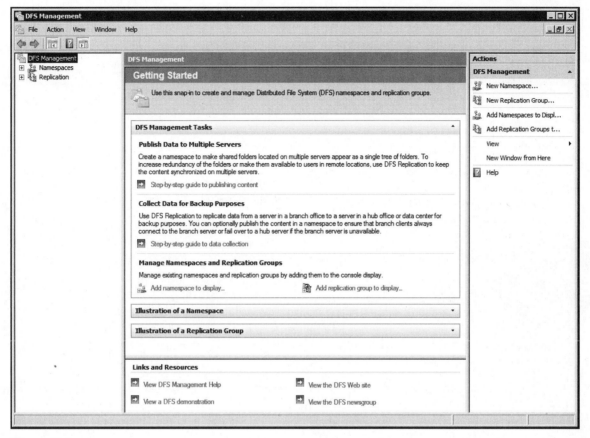

Figure 5-4
DFS Management console

2. Select the Namespaces node and, in the actions pane, click New Namespace. The New Namespace Wizard appears, displaying the *Namespace Server* page.

3. In the Server text box, key **Server##**, where ## is the number assigned to your server, and click Next. The *Namespace Name And Settings* page appears.

4. In the Name text box, key **Docs##**, where ## is the number assigned to your computer.

5. Click Edit Settings. The Edit Settings dialog box appears.

6. Select the Administrators have full access; other users have read and write permissions option, and click OK. Then click Next. The *Namespace Type* page appears.

7. Leave the Domain-based namespace option selected, and click Next. The *Review Settings and Create Namespace* page appears.

8. Click Create. The wizard creates the namespace.

9. Click Close. The Docs## namespace appears in the DFS Management console.

10. Leave the DFS Management console open for the next exercise.

Exercise 5.5	Adding a Folder to a Namespace
Overview	Once you have created a DFS namespace, you can add shared folders from any computer on the network, making them accessible through the namespace.
Completion time	10 minutes

1. In the DFS Management console, expand the Namespaces node, and select the Docs## namespace you created in Exercise 5.4.

> **NOTE**
>
> *Both your server and your partner server must have Exercise 5.4 completed in its entirety, with each server having its own DFS namespace, before you continue with Exercise 5.5. At the conclusion of Exercise 5.5, your server will have your partner server's share added to its namespace, and your partner server's namespace will have your share added to it.*

2. In the actions pane, select New Folder. The New Folder dialog box appears, as shown in Figure 5-5.

3. In the Name text box, key **Server ## Documents**.

4. Click Add. The Add Folder Target dialog box appears.

5. In the Path to folder target text box, key **Server##\Documents**, and click OK twice. The folder appears in the namespace.

6. Click New Folder to open the New Folder dialog box again.

7. Click Add to open the Add Folder Target dialog box.

8. Click Browse. The Browse for Shared Folders dialog box appears.

9. In the Server text box, key **Server##**, where ## is the number assigned to your partner server, and click Show Shared Folders.

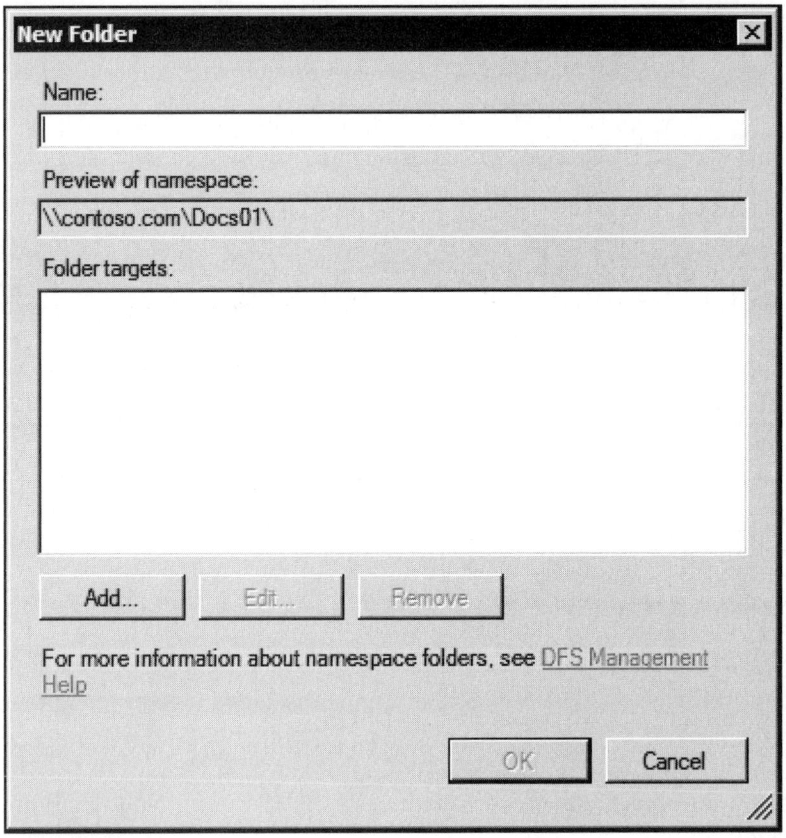

Figure 5-5
New Folder dialog box

Question 1	How many shared folders appear in the Browse for Shared Folders dialog box for your partner server? What are their names?

Question 2	How were the shares on your partner server created?

10. Select the Documents share, and click OK. The path to the share appears in the Add Folder Target dialog box.

11. Click OK. The share appears in the New Folder dialog box.

12. In the Name text box, key **Server## Documents**, where ## is the number assigned to your partner server, and then click OK. The new folder appears on the Namespace tab in the console.

13. Press Ctrl+Prt Scr to take a screen shot of the DFS Management console, showing both of the shared folders in your namespace, and then press Ctrl+V to paste the resulting image into the lab05_worksheet file in the page provided.

Question 3	On this domain-based namespace, where are the files stored that appear in the two Server## Documents folders?

14. Close the DFS Management console, and leave the computer logged on for the next exercise.

Exercise 5.6   Testing Namespace Access

Overview	To test a DFS namespace, you access it by using the server name and the name you specified during the namespace creation process.
Completion time	10 minutes

1. Open Windows Explorer, and browse to the X:\Docs folder you created in Exercise 5.3.

2. Right-click anywhere in the detail (right) pane and, from the context menu, select New > Folder.

3. Key **Statistics##**, where ## is the number assigned to your computer, and press Enter to name the folder.

4. Select the folder you created in the scope (left) pane, right-click anywhere in the detail pane and, from the context menu, select New > Rich Text Document.

5. Key **Budget##**, where ## is the number assigned to your computer, and press Enter to name the file.

6. Click Start, and then click Run. The Run dialog box appears.

7. In the Open text box, key **Server##\Docs##**, where ## is the number assigned to your partner server.

8. Click OK. An Explorer window appears, displaying the DFS namespace on your partner server.

Question 4	How many folders appear in the namespace?

9. Press Ctrl+Prt Scr to take a screen shot of the Explorer window, showing the namespace on your partner server and its folders, and then press Ctrl+V to paste the resulting image into the lab05_worksheet file in the page provided.

10. Open the Server## Documents folder named for your server, expand the Statistics folder, and double-click the Budget file to open it in Wordpad.

11. Key your name into the Budget file, and click File > Save.

Question 5	Which computer is hosting the DFS namspace you are currently accessing?

Question 6	On which computer are you saving the modified version of the Budget file?

12. In Windows Explorer, open the C:\DfsRoots\Docs## folder.

13. Double-click the Server## Documents folder, named for your partner server.

Question 7	What happens?

14. Double-click the Server## Documents folder, named for your own server.

Question 8	What happens this time?

Question 9	How can you explain these results?

15. Close the two Explorer windows, and leave the server logged on for the next exercise.

Exercise 5.7	Adding a Namespace Server
Overview	One of the advantages of a domain-based DFS namespace is the ability to designate multiple namespace servers for fault tolerance purposes.
Completion time	10 minutes

1. Open the Run dialog box. In the Open text box, key **contoso.com\Docs##**, where ## is the number assigned to your server, and then click OK. An Explorer window appears, displaying the Docs## namespace you created.

Question 10	Where are the target folders for this namespace, which you are seeing in the Explorer window, currently being stored?

2. Shut down your partner server for a few minutes (or ask your lab partner to shut it down).

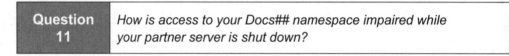

During this exercise, if you are working with a lab partner, you will have to take turns shutting down your servers momentarily and using each other's servers to access your namespaces.

3.   Try to open the two Server## Documents folders on your Docs## namespace.

> **Question 11**   *How is access to your Docs## namespace impaired while your partner server is shut down?*

4.   Start up your partner server again, and shut down your own server.

5.   At your partner server, log on using your Student## account and the password *P@ssw0rd*.

6.   Try to access your Docs## namespace by opening the \\contoso.com\Docs## path from the Run dialog box.

> **Question 12**   *How is access to your Docs## namespace affected while your server is shut down?*

7.   Log off of your partner server, and restart your own server.

8.   Log on to your server using your Student## account and the password *P@ssw0rd*.

9.   Open the DFS Management console, and expand the Namespaces node.

10.   Select the Docs## namespace you created in Exercise 5.4 and, in the actions pane, click Add Namespace Server. The Add Namespace Server dialog box appears, as shown in Figure 5-6.

11.   In the Namespace server text box, key the name of your partner server, **Server##**.

12.   Click Edit Settings. The Edit Settings dialog box appears.

13.   Select the Administrators have full access; other users have read and write permissions option, and click OK. Then, in the Add Namespace Server dialog box, click OK again.

14.   In the DFS Management console, select the Namespace Servers tab.

15.   Press Ctrl+Prt Scr to take a screen shot of the DFS Management console, showing the two namespace servers in your Docs## namespace, and then press Ctrl+V to paste the resulting image into the lab05_worksheet file in the page provided.

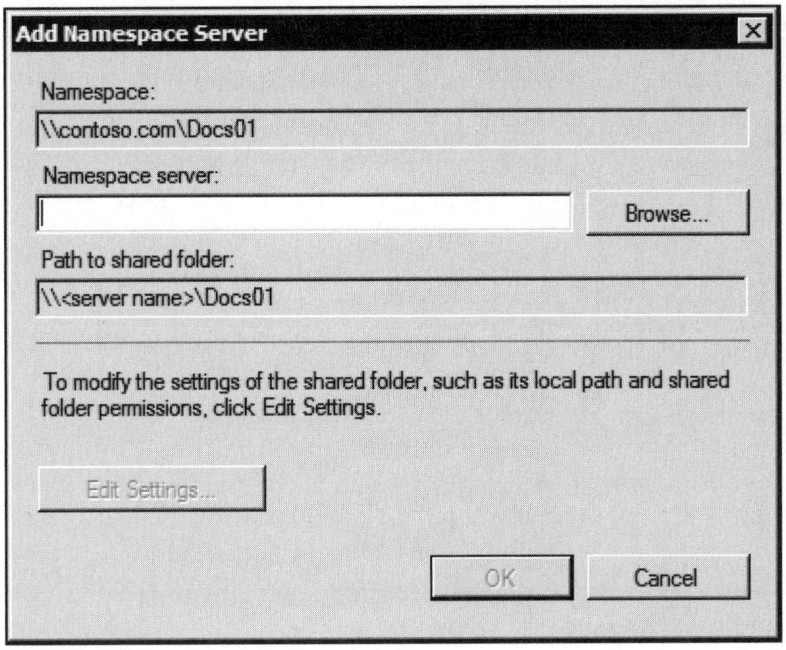

Figure 5-6
Add Namespace Server dialog box

16. Shut down your server, and try again to access the two folders in your Docs## namespace from your partner server.

Question 13	*What is the result now? Explain why the results are different from your previous attempt.*

17. Restart your server.

Exercise 5.8	**Installing a Printer**
Overview	On your test network, you are examining the capabilities of the Print Management console included in Windows Server 2008. In this exercise, you use the Print Management console to install some test printers.
Completion time	10 minutes

1. Log on using your Student## account and the password *P@ssw0rd*.

2. Close the Initial Configuration Tasks window when it appears.

3. Click Start, and then click Administrative Tools > Print Management. After you click Continue in the User Account Control message box, the Print Management console appears, as shown in Figure 5-7.

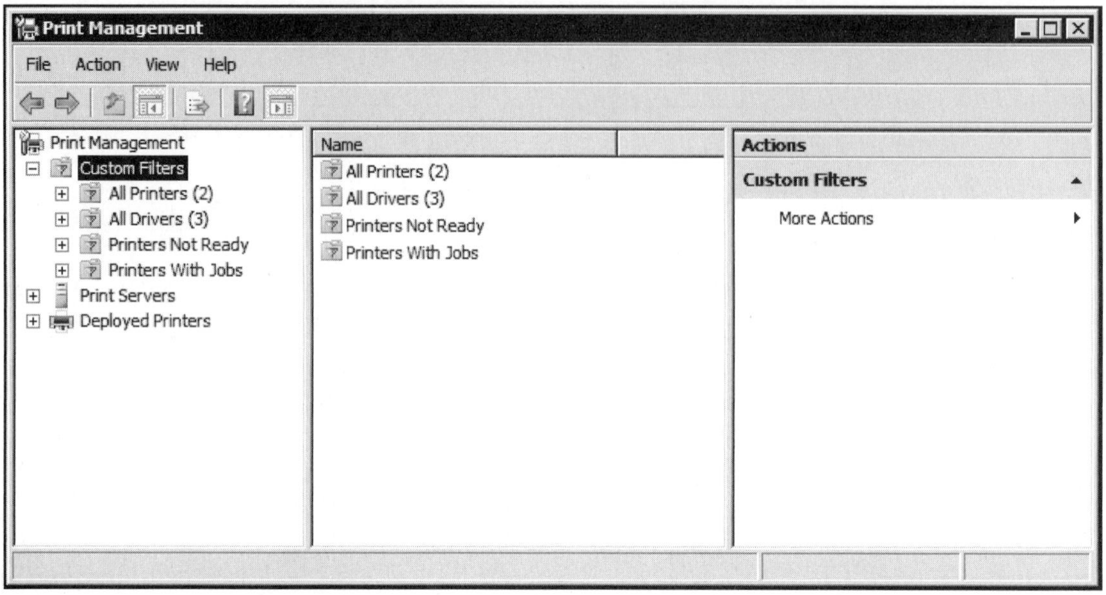

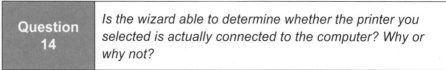

Figure 5-7
Print Management console

4. Expand the Print Servers node, and then right-click the Server## (local) node, representing your computer. From the context menu, select Add Printer. The Network Printer Installation Wizard appears.

5. Select the Add a new printer using an existing port option. Leave the LPT1: (Printer Port) value selected, and then click Next. The *Printer Driver* page appears.

6. Leave the Install a new driver option selected, and click Next. The *Printer Installation* page appears.

7. In the Manufacturer list, select Generic.

8. In the Printers list, select MS Publisher Color Printer, and click Next. The *Printer Name and Sharing Settings* page appears.

9. In the Printer Name text box, key **MSColor##**, where ## is the number assigned to your computer.

10. Leave the Share this printer checkbox selected. In the Share Name text box, key **MSColor##**, and then click Next. The *Printer Found* page appears.

Question 14	*Is the wizard able to determine whether the printer you selected is actually connected to the computer? Why or why not?*

11. Click Next. The *Completing the Network Printer Installation Wizard* page appears.

12. Once the printer is installed, click Finish.

13. Repeat the process to install a second printer, using the following settings:

    - Port: LPT2
    - Manufacturer: Generic
    - Printer: MS Publisher Imagesetter
    - Printer Name: MSMono##, where ## is the number assigned to your computer
    - Share Name: MSMono##, where ## is the number assigned to your computer

14. Select the Printers node under your particular print server in the Print Management console.

15. Press Ctrl+Prt Scr to take a screen shot of the Print Management console, showing the contents of the Printers node, and then press Ctrl+V to paste the resulting image into the lab05_worksheet file in the page provided.

16. Leave the Print Management console open for the next exercise.

Exercise 5.9	Deploying Printers Using Active Directory
Overview	To simplify future network printer deployments, your company plans to publish printer connections using Active Directory and Group Policy. In this execise, you deploy the printers you created in two different ways.
Completion time	10 minutes

1. In the Print Management console, expand the node representing your server, and select the Printers node beneath it.

2. Right-click the MSColor## printer and, from the context menu, select List In Directory.

3. Right-click the MSMono## printer and, from the context menu, select Deploy with Group Policy. The Deploy with Group Policy dialog box appears, as shown in Figure 5-8.

4. Click Browse. The Browse For A Group Policy Object dialog box appears.

5. Select Default Domain Policy, and click OK. Default Domain Policy appears in the GPO Name field.

6. Select the The computers that this GPO applies to (per machine) checkbox, and click Add.

7. Click OK. A Print Management message box appears, indicating that the printer deployment has succeeded.

8. Click OK to close the message box, and click OK again to close the Deploy with Group Policy dialog box.

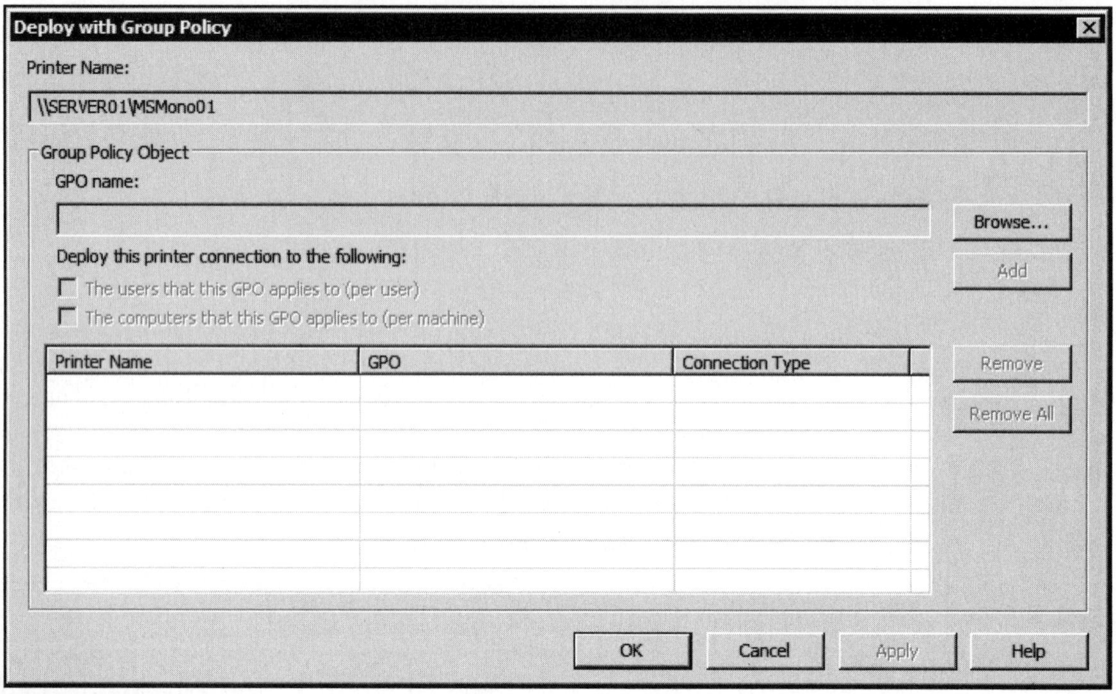

Figure 5-8
Deploy with Group Policy dialog box

9. When this exercise is completed to this point on your partner server, restart your computer.

10. When your computer restarts, log on using your Student## account and the password *P@ssw0rd*.

11. Click Start, and then click Control Panel.

12. Double-click the Printers icon. The Printers window appears.

Question 15	Apart from Microsoft XPS Document Writer, which appears by default, which of your partner server's printers appear in the window?

Question 16	Why doesn't your partner server's MSColor## printer appear in the Printers window?

13. Click Start, and then click Network. The Network window appears.

14. Click Search Active Directory. The Find Users, Contacts, and Groups dialog box appears.

15. In the Find drop-down list, select Printers. The title of the dialog box changes to Find Printers.

16. Click Find Now.

Question 17	*What printers appear in the Search Results box?*

17. Right-click your partner server's MSColor## printer and, from the context menu, select Connect.

18. Switch to the Printers window.

Question 18	*What has changed in the Printers window?*

19. Press Ctrl+Prt Scr to take a screen shot of the Printers window, and then press Ctrl+V to paste the resulting image into the lab05_worksheet file in the page provided.

20. Close the Printers window and the Network window.

21. Log off of the computer.

LAB REVIEW QUESTIONS

Completion time	10 minutes

1. In Exercise 5.2, you used the Sharing and Storage Management console to create a simple volume. What must you do to create a different volume type such as a mirrored, striped, or RAID-5 volume?

2. In Exercise 5.7, you accessed a DFS namespace using the Contoso domain name. One reason for creating a domain-based namespace instead of a standalone namespace is to suppress the server name in the namespace path. Why is suppressing the server name considered an advantage?

3. In Exercise 5.6, you accessed the DFS namespace on your partner server and modified a file called Budget. Explain why the file you modified was actually stored on your own server and not the partner server.

4. In Exercise 5.4 when you created a domain-based namespace, the Enable Windows Server 2008 mode checkbox on the *Namespace Type* page was selected by default. Under what circumstances would this checkbox be grayed out?

LAB CHALLENGE: CONFIGURING DFS REPLICATION

Completion time	20 minutes

In Exercise 5.7, you added a second namespace server to your domain-based namespace so that if one of the servers fails, the namespace still remains available. However, even though the namespace would remain available in the event of a server failure, one of the shared folders in the namespace would not be available. To make the data folders in the namespace fault tolerant as well, you can use DFS Replication to duplicate each folder on the other server.

To complete this challenge, use the DFS Management console to configure your Docs## namespace to be fully fault tolerant by using DFS Replication so that all resources remain available when one of the two servers fails. List the steps for the procedure you use to configure the namespace. Press Ctrl+Prt Scr to take a screen shot of the DFS Management console, demonstrating that the Docs## namespace is using DFS Replication, and then press Ctrl+V to paste the resulting image into the lab05_worksheet file in the page provided.

> **NOTE**
> *To avoid conflicts with your partner server, do not use the same folder name when replicating your folders to the other server. For example, if you were replicating a folder called Data01 to your partner server, you might call the folder Data01a.*

WORKSTATION RESET: RETURNING TO BASELINE

Completion time	10 minutes

To return the computer to its baseline state, complete the following procedures.

1. Open the DFS Management console, and delete the Docs## namespace you created, along with its folders.

2. Open the Share and Storage Management console, and delete the Documents share you created.

3. Open the Server Manager console, and remove the File Services and Print Services roles as well as the installed printers.

LAB 6
WORKING WITH DISKS

This lab contains the following exercises and activities:

BEFORE YOU BEGIN

The classroom network consists of Windows Server 2008 student servers that are all connected to a local area network. There is also a classroom server, named ServerDC, that is connected to the same classroom network. ServerDC is also running Windows Server 2008 and is the domain controller for a domain named contoso.com. Throughout the labs in this manual, you will be working with the same student server on which you will install, configure, maintain, and troubleshoot application roles, features, and services.

Your instructor should have supplied you with the information needed to fill in the following table:

Student computer name (Server##)	
Student account name (Student##)	

Working with Lab Worksheets

Each lab in this manual requires that you answer questions, shoot screen shots, or perform other activities that you are to document in a worksheet named for the lab, such as lab01_worksheet. Your instructor will supply you with the worksheet files by copying them to the Students\Worksheets share on ServerDC. As you perform the exercises in each lab, open the appropriate worksheet file using WordPad, fill in the required information, and save the file to your computer's Student##\Documents folder. This folder is automatically redirected to the ServerDC computer. Your instructor will examine these worksheet files to assess your performance.

The procedure for opening and saving a worksheet file is as follows:

1. Click Start, and then click Run. The Run dialog box appears.

2. In the Open text box, key **\\ServerDC\Students\Worksheets\lab##_worksheet** (where lab## contains the number of the lab you're completing), and click OK.

3. The worksheet document opens in Wordpad.

4. Complete all of the exercises in the worksheet.

5. In WordPad, choose Save As from the File menu. The Save As dialog box appears.

6. In the File Name text box, key **lab##_worksheet_*yourname*** (where lab## contains the number of the lab you're completing and *yourname* is your last name), and click Save.

SCENARIO

You are a server administrator working in a medium-sized organization. One morning, Karen, the manager of the Accounting department, calls to complain that she created an important document file yesterday and saved it to her departmental server, and now she can't find it. Karen goes on to explain that this sort of thing happens to her all the time; she creates files and saves them, and when she tries to open them again later, she has to spend half an hour looking for them. Sometimes she finds the file she needs, and sometimes she doesn't and is forced to create it all over again.

Because of the sensitivity of the data stored there, Karen insists on managing the Accounting server herself. When she allows you to examine the server drives, you find document files strewn about in folders everywhere, some intermixed with application files and others stored in the volume root. You decide to show Karen the basics of file management, starting with creating a new volume for the department's data files to keep them separate from the application and operating system files.

After completing this lab, you will be able to:

■ Use the Disk Management snap-in to create and manage storage volumes

■ Use the Diskpart.exe utility to create storage volumes

Estimated lab time: 110 minutes

Exercise 6.1	Creating a Simple Volume
Overview	Thanks to your instruction, Karen now sees the advantage of storing the department's data files on a volume separate from the operating system and application files. In this exercise, you create a new simple volume on the server where the accountants can store their data.
Completion time	10 minutes

1. Turn on your computer. When the logon screen appears, log on using your Student## account and the password *P@ssw0rd*.

2. Close the Initial Configuration Tasks window when it appears.

3. Click Start, and then click Administrative Tools > Computer Management. Click Continue in the User Account Control message box, and the Computer Management console appears.

4. In the scope (left) pane, click Disk Management. The Disk Management snap-in appears in the detail (right) pane, as shown in Figure 6-1.

5. Based on the information in the Disk Management snap-in, fill out the information in Table 6-1 on your lab worksheet.

Table 6-1
Disk Information

	Disk 0	*Disk 1*
Disk type (basic or dynamic)		
Total disk size		
Number and type of partitions		
Amount of unallocated space		

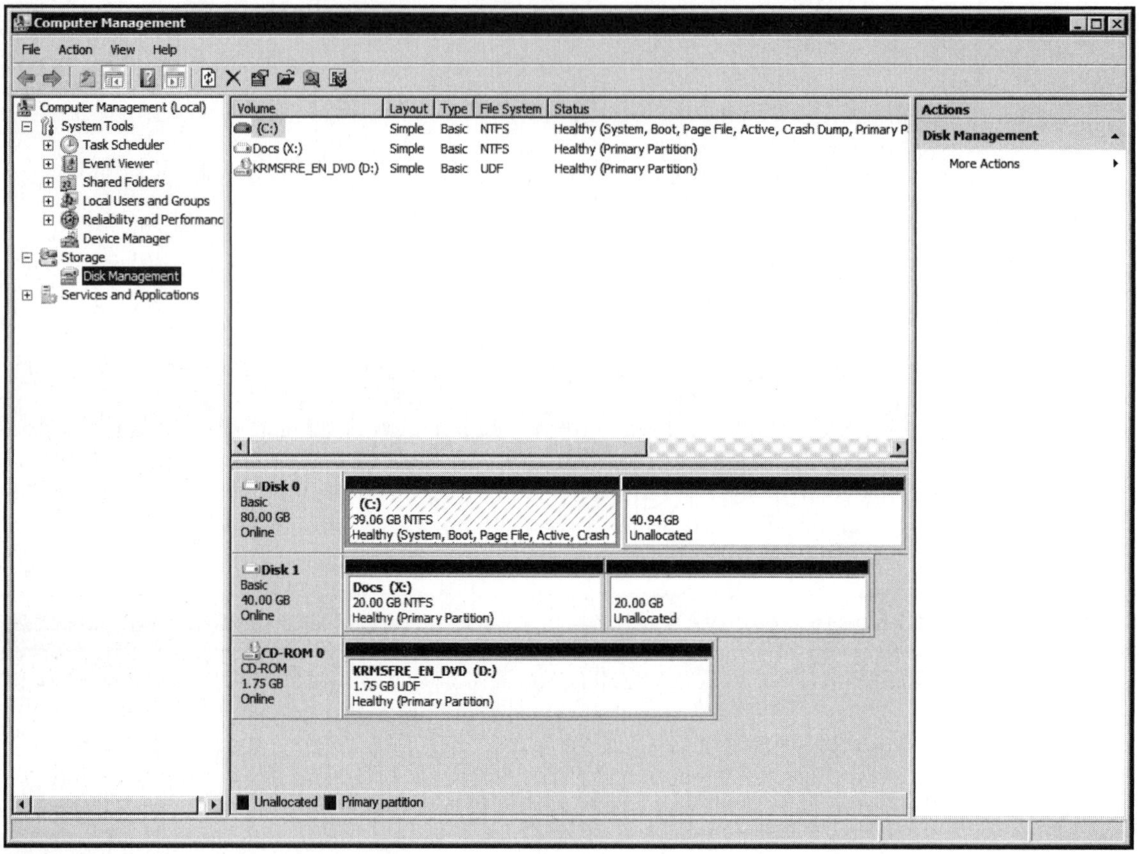

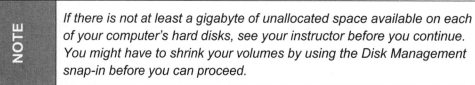

Figure 6-1
Disk Management snap-in

> **NOTE**
>
> *If there is not at least a gigabyte of unallocated space available on each of your computer's hard disks, see your instructor before you continue. You might have to shrink your volumes by using the Disk Management snap-in before you can proceed.*

6. In the graphical display in the bottom pane, right-click the Unallocated area of Disk 0 and, from the context menu, select New Simple Volume. The New Simple Volume Wizard appears.

7. Click Next to bypass the Welcome page. The *Specify Volume Size* page appears.

8. In the Simple volume size in MB text box, key **1000**, and click Next. The *Assign Drive Letter or Path* page appears.

9. Leave the Assign the following drive letter option selected. Choose drive letter S from the drop-down list, and then click Next. The *Format Partition* page appears.

10. Leave the Format this volume with the following settings option selected, and configure the next three parameters as follows:

  • File System: NTFS
  • Allocation Unit Size: Default
  • Volume Label: **Karen1**

11. Select the Perform a quick format checkbox, and click Next. The *Completing the New Simple Volume Wizard* page appears.

12. Click Finish. The new volume appears in the Disk Management snap-in.

13. Press Ctrl+Prt Scr to take a screen shot of the Disk Management snap-in, showing the volume you created, and then press Ctrl+V to paste the resulting image into the lab06_worksheet file in the page provided.

14. Leave the Computer Management console open for future exercises.

Exercise 6.2	Extending a Volume
Overview	A few days later, you receive another call from Karen. She has been diligently moving the department's data files to the volume you created for her, but she has now run out of disk space. The volume was not big enough! To address the problem, you decide to extend the Karen1 volume by using some of the unallocated space left on the disk. For this task, you intend to use the Diskpart.exe command line utility.
Completion time	15 minutes

1. Click Start, and then click All Programs > Accessories > Windows Explorer.

2. In the folders pane, expand the Computer container, and locate the S: drive you created in Exercise 6-1.

3. Right-click the S: drive and, from the context menu, select New > Folder. Give the new folder the name **WinSvr2008**.

4. Click Start, and then click Run. The Run dialog box appears.

5. In the Open text box, key **\\serverdc\install\WinSvr2008**, and click OK. A second Explorer window appears, displaying the contents of the WinSvr2008 folder on the classroom server, as shown in Figure 6-2.

6. Select the entire contents of the WinSvr2008 folder on ServerDC, and drag it to the S:\WinSvr2008 folder you created on your computer.

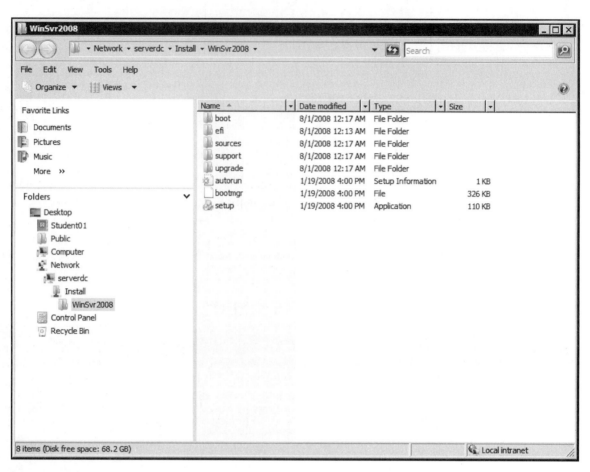

Figure 6-2
WinSvr2008 folder on ServerDC

Question 1	*What is the result?*

7. Click Cancel.

8. Consult the Disk Management snap-in, and fill out Table 6-2 with the amount of unallocated space left on the drives in gigabytes and megabytes.

The best way to determine the amount of space is to right-click on each unallocated space, select Properties, and then select the Volumes tab.

Table 6-2
Unallocated Space Remaining

	Disk 0	Disk 1
Unallocated space left (gigabytes)		
Unallocated space left (megabytes)		

9. Open the Run dialog box. In the Open text box, key **diskpart**, and press Enter. Click Continue in the User Account Control message box, and a Command Prompt window appears containing the DISKPART> prompt.

10. Key **select disk 0**, and press Enter. The program responds, saying that Disk 0 is now the selected disk.

11. Key **list partition**, and press Enter. A list of the partitions on Disk 0 appears.

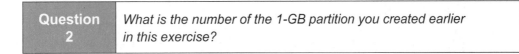

Question 2	What is the number of the 1-GB partition you created earlier in this exercise?

12. Key **select partition #**, where # is the number of the 1-GB partition, and press Enter. The program responds, saying that Partition # is now the selected partition.

13. Key **extend size = *xxxx***, where *xxxx* is the amount of unallocated space left on the drive, in megabytes, from Table 6-2. Then, press Enter.

Question 3	What is the result?

14. Press Ctrl+Prt Scr to take a screen shot of the Disk Management snap-in, showing the extended volume, and then press Ctrl+V to paste the resulting image into the lab06_worksheet file in the page provided.

15. In the Diskpart window, key **exit**, and press Enter to terminate the Diskpart program.

16. Try again to copy the entire contents of the WinSvr2008 folder on ServerDC to the S:\WinSvr2008 folder on your computer.

Question 4	What is the result?

17. Leave the Disk Management snap-in open for the next exercise.

Exercise 6.3	Creating Additional Volumes
Overview	Karen is thrilled at the idea of storing her department's data files in separate volumes, and now she wants you to create more partitions on her server. However, you used all of the available space to create her Karen1 volume. Therefore, you have to shrink the Karen1 volume to create room for the additional volumes she wants.
Completion time	10 minutes

1. In the Disk Management snap-in, right-click the Karen1 volume you created on Disk 0 and, from the context menu, select Shrink Volume. The Shrink S: dialog box appears, as shown in Figure 6-3.

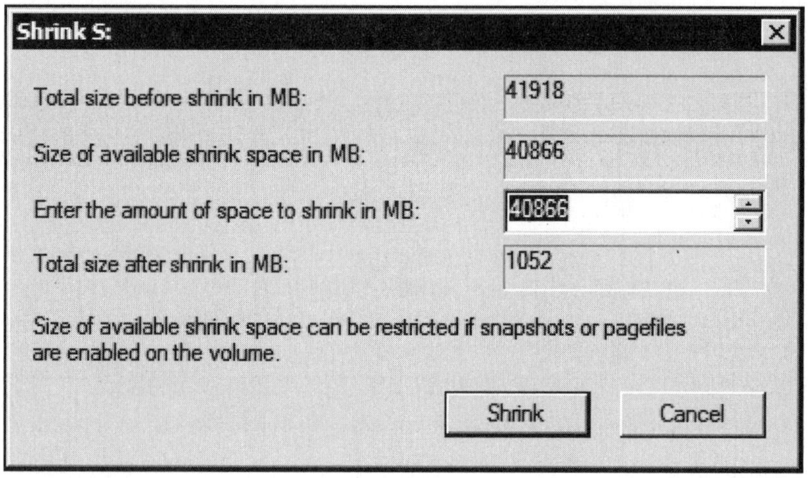

Shrink S:

Total size before shrink in MB:	41918
Size of available shrink space in MB:	40866
Enter the amount of space to shrink in MB:	40866
Total size after shrink in MB:	1052

Size of available shrink space can be restricted if snapshots or pagefiles are enabled on the volume.

[Shrink] [Cancel]

Figure 6-3
Shrink S: dialog box

Question 5	*How much available shrink space is contained in the volume?*

2. In the Enter the amount of space to shrink in MB spin box, key the amount of available shrink space minus 2000 MB (2 GB).

3. Click Shrink. The amount of space you entered appears as unallocated space in the Disk Management snap-in.

4. Right-click the unallocated space in Disk 0, and select New Simple Volume. The New Simple Volume Wizard appears.

5. Use the wizard to create a new 2000-MB partition, using the drive letter T, the NTFS file system, the volume name **Karen2**, and the Quick Format option.

6. Repeat steps 4 and 5 to create another 2000-MB partition, using the drive letter U, the NTFS file system, and the volume name **Karen3**.

Question 6	*How is the last volume you created different from the previous ones? Explain why.*

Question 7	*What do you suppose would happen if you created another simple volume out of the free space left on the disk?*

7. Press Ctrl+Prt Scr to take a screen shot of the Disk Management snap-in, showing the volumes you created, and then press Ctrl+V to paste the resulting image into the lab06_worksheet file in the page provided.

8. Leave the Computer Management console open for the next exercise.

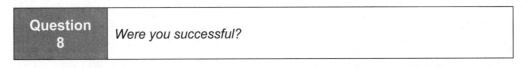

Exercise 6.4   Mounting a Volume

Overview	Karen calls yet again to tell you that she needs still more space on her Karen1 volume, but is unable to expand it. You decide to provide her with additional space by creating a volume and mounting it in a folder on the Karen1 volume.
Completion time	15 minutes

1. In the Disk Management snap-in, right-click the Karen1 volume you created in Exercise 6.1, and try to extend it by 2000 MB.

Question 8	*Were you successful?*

2. Right-click the Karen3 volume you created in Exercise 6.3 and, from the context menu, select Extend Volume. The Extend Volume Wizard appears.

3. Click Next to bypass the Welcome page. The *Select Disks* page appears, as shown in Figure 6-4.

4. In the Select the amount of space in MB spin box, key **2000**, and click Next. The *Completing the Extend Volume Wizard* page appears.

5. Click Finish.

Question 9	*What is the result?*

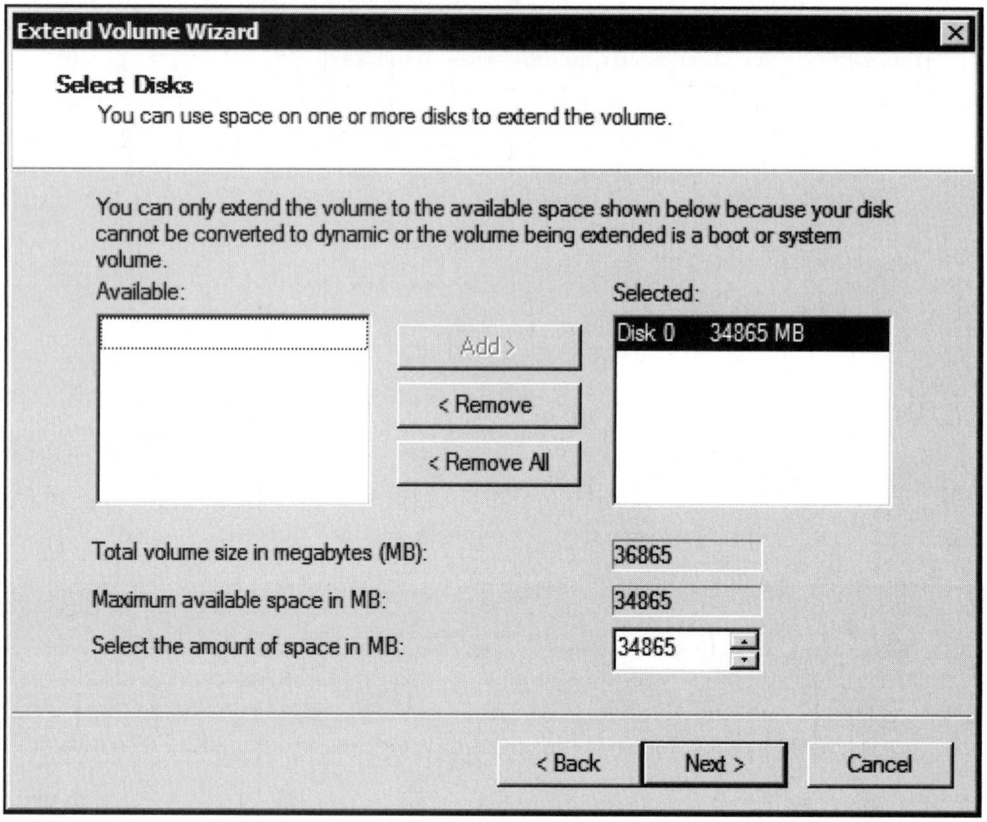

Figure 6-4
Select Disks page of the Extend Volume Wizard

6. Open Windows Explorer, and create a new folder on the computer's S: drive named **Karen4**.

7. In the Disk Management snap-in, right-click the remaining Free Space element on Disk 0 and, from the context menu, select New Simple Volume. The New Simple Volume Wizard appears.

8. On the *Specify Volume Size* page, specify a volume size of **2000** MB, and then click Next.

9. On the *Assign Drive Letter or Path* page, select the Mount in the following empty NTFS folder option. In the text box, key **S:\Karen4**, and click Next.

10. On the *Format Partition* page, select the NTFS file system and, in the Volume label text box, key **Karen4**.

11. Select the Perform a quick format checkbox, and click Next.

12. Click Finish to create the volume.

13. Press Ctrl+Prt Scr to take a screen shot of the Disk Management snap-in, showing the volumes you created, and then press Ctrl+V to paste the resulting image into the lab06_worksheet file in the page provided.

14. In Windows Explorer, right-click the S: drive and, from the context menu, select Properties. The Karen1 (S:) Properties sheet appears.

15. Fill out Table 6-3 with the amount of used, free, and total space on the S: drive in gigabytes and megabytes.

Table 6-3
Karen1 (S:) Properties

	Megabytes	Gigabytes
Used space		
Free space		
Capacity		

Question 10	Does the capacity of the S: drive reflect the addition of the mounted Karen4 volume?

16. Click OK to close the Karen1 (S:) Properties sheet.

17. Select the S:\Karen4 icon.

NOTE	If the status bar does not appear at the bottom of the Windows Explorer window, activate it by selecting Status Bar from the View menu.

Question 11	According to the status bar, how much free space is on the Karen4 volume?

Question 12	Does the free space on Karen4 reflect the space available on the Karen1 volume as well?

18. Close all Windows Explorer windows.

19. Leave the Computer Management console open for the next exercise.

Exercise 6.5   Removing Volumes

Overview	The Accounting department server currently has five volumes on its disk: three primary partitions and one extended partition with two logical drives. Karen and her staff have found it difficult to manage their files with so many volumes, so she wants to consolidate the disk into just two volumes: her original volume, plus one large data volume, which will be a spanned volume that uses all of the available space on Disk 0 plus all of the space on the second hard disk in the computer.
Completion time	10 minutes

1.   In the Disk Management snap-in, right-click the Karen4 volume and, from the context menu, select Delete Volume. A Delete Simple Volume message box appears, warning you that deleting the volume will erase all of the data stored on it.

2.   Click Yes. The volume is deleted.

3.   Repeat steps 1 and 2 to delete the Karen3 volume.

Question 13	Why doesn't the disk space used by the Karen3 and Karen4 volumes appear in the Disk Management snap-in as unallocated?

4.   Repeat steps 1 and 2 to delete the Karen2 volume.

5.   Right-click the Karen1 volume and, from the context menu, select Extend Volume. The Extend Volume Wizard appears.

6.   Click Next to bypass the Welcome page. The *Select Disks* page appears.

Question 14	What is the maximum amount of space that you can use to extend the Karen1 volume?

Question 15	Why can't you extend the Karen1 volume by using all of the remaining space on the disk?

7.   Click Cancel to close the wizard.

8.   Repeat steps 1 and 2 to delete all of the volumes on both of the computer's disks, including the extended partition on Disk 0, except for the original C: volume and the Karen1 volume you created in Exercise 6.1.

9.   Leave the Disk Management snap-in open for the next exercise.

Exercise 6.6	Creating a Spanned Volume
Overview	Now that you have deleted the extra volumes on the Accounting server, you can extend the Karen1 volume to use all of the disk space on both of the computer's hard drives.
Completion time	10 minutes

1. In the Disk Management snap-in, right-click the Karen1 volume and, from the context menu, select Extend Volume. The Extend Volume Wizard appears.

2. Click Next to bypass the Welcome page. The *Select Disks* page appears.

Question 16	What is the maximum amount of space that you can use to extend the Karen1 volume?

Question 17	Why can't you extend the Karen1 volume to the second hard disk (Disk 1)?

3. Press Ctrl+Prt Scr to take a screen shot of the *Select Disks* page, and then press Ctrl+V to paste the resulting image into the lab06_worksheet file in the page provided.

4. Click Cancel to close the wizard.

5. Right-click the Disk 0 box and, from the context menu, select Convert to Dynamic Disk. The Convert to Dynamic Disk dialog box appears, as shown in Figure 6-5.

6. Select both the Disk 0 and Disk 1 checkboxes, and click OK. The Disks to Convert dialog box appears.

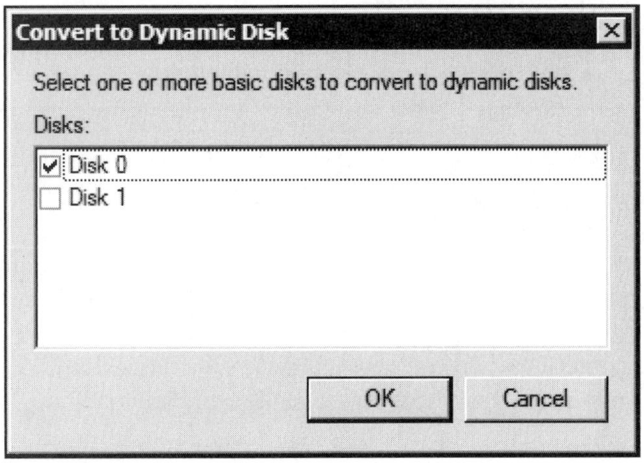

Figure 6-5
Convert to Dynamic Disk dialog box

7. Click Convert. A Disk Management message box appears, warning you that you cannot dual-boot a computer from a dynamic disk.

8. Click Yes. Both of the disks are converted from basic to dynamic disks.

9. Once again, right-click the Karen1 volume and, from the context menu, select Extend Volume. The Extend Volume Wizard appears.

10. Click Next to bypass the Welcome page. The *Select Disks* page appears.

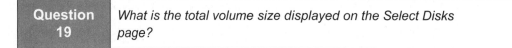

Question 18	How is the Select Disks page different now that you have converted the basic disks to dynamic disks?

11. Select Disk 1 in the Available box, and click Add. Disk 1 moves to the Selected box.

Question 19	What is the total volume size displayed on the Select Disks page?

12. Click Next. The *Completing the Extend Volume Wizard* page appears.

13. Click Finish. The Karen1 volume expands to encompass all of the available space on both disks.

14. Press Ctrl+Prt Scr to take a screen shot of the Disk Management snap-in, showing the spanned volume you created, and then press Ctrl+V to paste the resulting image into the lab06_worksheet file in the page provided.

15. Close the Computer Management console, and log off of the computer.

LAB REVIEW QUESTIONS

Completion time	10 minutes

1. In Exercise 6.5, why doesn't the extended partition you created appear in the Disk Management snap-in's volume list in the top view pane?

2. In Exercise 6.4, why is it that you were unable to extend the Karen1 volume and were forced to mount a volume to a folder instead, but you were able to extend Karen3?

3. In Exercise 6.6 after you converted Disk 0 from a basic disk to a dynamic disk, how many partitions were there on the disk? How do you know?

4. If one of the hard disk drives should fail after creating the spanned volume on the Accounting server by using space from both hard disks, what would happen to the data stored on the volume?

LAB CHALLENGE: CREATING A STRIPED VOLUME

Completion time	20 minutes

Karen wants to increase the disk performance on her server and has decided that, instead of a single spanned volume, she wants to create a single striped volume as large as her server can support. To complete this challenge, delete the Karen1 spanned volume, and re-create it as a striped volume using the same file system and formatting parameters. To complete these tasks, you can use only the Diskpart.exe utility. List the Diskpart commands you used. When you are finished, open the Disk Management snap-in, and press Ctrl+Prt Scr to take a screen shot, showing the striped volume you created. Then, press Ctrl+V to paste the resulting image into the lab06_worksheet file in the page provided.

WORKSTATION RESET: RETURNING TO BASELINE

Completion time	10 minutes

To return the computer to its baseline state, complete the following procedure.

1. Open the Disk Management snap-in.

2. Delete all of the volumes on both disks except for the original C: volume that contains the operating system.

LAB 7
USING HIGH-AVAILABILITY FEATURES

This lab contains the following exercises and activities:

BEFORE YOU BEGIN

The classroom network consists of Windows Server 2008 student servers that are all connected to a local area network. There is also a classroom server, named ServerDC, that is

connected to the same classroom network. ServerDC is also running Windows Server 2008 and is the domain controller for a domain named contoso.com. Throughout the labs in this manual, you will be working with the same student server on which you will install, configure, maintain, and troubleshoot application roles, features, and services.

Your instructor should have supplied you with the information needed to fill in the following table:

Student computer name (Server##)	
Student account name (Student##)	

To complete the exercises in this lab, you will require access to a second student computer on the classroom network, referred to in the exercises as your *partner server*. Depending on the configuration of your network, use one of the following options as directed by your instructor:

- For a conventional classroom network with one operating system installed on each computer, you must have a lab partner with his or her own computer, performing the same exercises as yourself.

- For a classroom in which each computer uses local virtualization software to install multiple operating systems, you must run two virtual machines representing student computers and perform the exercises separately on each virtual machine.

- For a classroom that uses online virtualization, you will have access to two virtual student servers in your Web browser. You must perform the exercises separately on each virtual machine.

Working with Lab Worksheets

Each lab in this manual requires that you answer questions, shoot screen shots, or perform other activities that you are to document in a worksheet named for the lab, such as lab01_worksheet. Your instructor will supply you with the worksheet files by copying them to the Students\Worksheets share on ServerDC. As you perform the exercises in each lab, open the appropriate worksheet file using WordPad, fill in the required information, and save the file to your computer's Student##\Documents folder. This folder is automatically redirected to the ServerDC computer. Your instructor will examine these worksheet files to assess your performance.

The procedure for opening and saving a worksheet file is as follows:

1. Click Start, and then click Run. The Run dialog box appears.

2. In the Open text box, key **\\ServerDC\Students\Worksheets\lab##_worksheet** (where lab## contains the number of the lab you're completing), and click OK.

3. The worksheet document opens in WordPad.

4. Complete all of the exercises in the worksheet.

5. In WordPad, choose Save As from the File menu. The Save As dialog box appears.

6. In the File Name text box, key **lab##_worksheet_*yourname*** (where lab## contains the number of the lab you're completing and *yourname* is your last name), and click Save.

SCENARIO

You are a server administrator working in the IT test lab in a medium-sized organization. After a recent server hardware failure that stopped production for several hours, your supervisor has instructed you to look into the various high-availability technologies built into Windows Server 2008.

After completing this lab, you will be able to:

■ Configure and use Shadow Copies

■ Create a Network Load Balancing cluster

■ Create a failover cluster

Estimated lab time: 140 minutes

Exercise 7.1	Creating a Volume
Overview	Shadow Copies is a Windows Server 2008 feature that enables end-users to access previous versions of their documents without IT intervention. To test Shadow Copies, you must first create a volume on your lab server and populate it with files.
Completion time	10 minutes

1. Turn on your computer. When the logon screen appears, log on using your Student## account and the password *P@ssw0rd*.

2. Close the Initial Configuration Tasks window when it appears.

3. Click Start, and then click Administrative Tools > Computer Management. Click Continue in the User Account Control message box, and the Computer Management console appears.

4. In the scope (left) pane, click Disk Management. The Disk Management snap-in appears.

5. Right-click the Unallocated area of Disk 0 and, from the context menu, select New Simple Volume. The New Simple Volume Wizard appears.

6. Click Next to bypass the Welcome page. The *Specify Volume Size* page appears.

7. Click Next to accept the maximum value for the Simple volume size in MB text box. The *Assign Drive Letter or Path* page appears.

8. Leave the Assign the following drive letter option selected, choose drive letter X from the drop-down list, and then click Next. The *Format Partition* page appears.

9. Leave the Format this volume with the following settings option selected, and configure the next three parameters as follows:

    - File System: NTFS
    - Allocation Unit Size: Default
    - Volume Label: Data

10. Select the Perform a quick format checkbox, and click Next. The *Completing the New Simple Volume Wizard* page appears.

11. Click Finish. The new volume appears in the Disk Management snap-in.

12. Close the Disk Management console.

13. Click Start, and then click All Programs > Accessories > Windows Explorer.

14. In the folders pane, expand the Computer container, and locate the X: drive you created.

15. Right-click the X: drive and, from the context menu, select New > Folder. Give the new folder the name **WinSvr2008**.

16. Click Start, and then click Run. The Run dialog box appears.

17. In the Open text box, key **\\serverdc\install\WinSvr2008**, and click OK. A second Explorer window appears, displaying the contents of the WinSvr2008 folder on the classroom server.

18. Select the entire contents of the WinSvr2008 folder on ServerDC, and drag it to the X:\WinSvr2008 folder you created on your computer.

19. Leave Windows Explorer open for the next exercise.

Exercise 7.2	Configuring Shadow Copies
Overview	To use Shadow Copies, you must configure the feature on each server volume you want to protect.
Completion time	15 minutes

1. In Windows Explorer, right-click the Data (X:) volume and, from the context menu, select Configure Shadow Copies. Click Continue in the User Account Control message box, and the Shadow Copies dialog box appears, as shown in Figure 7-1.

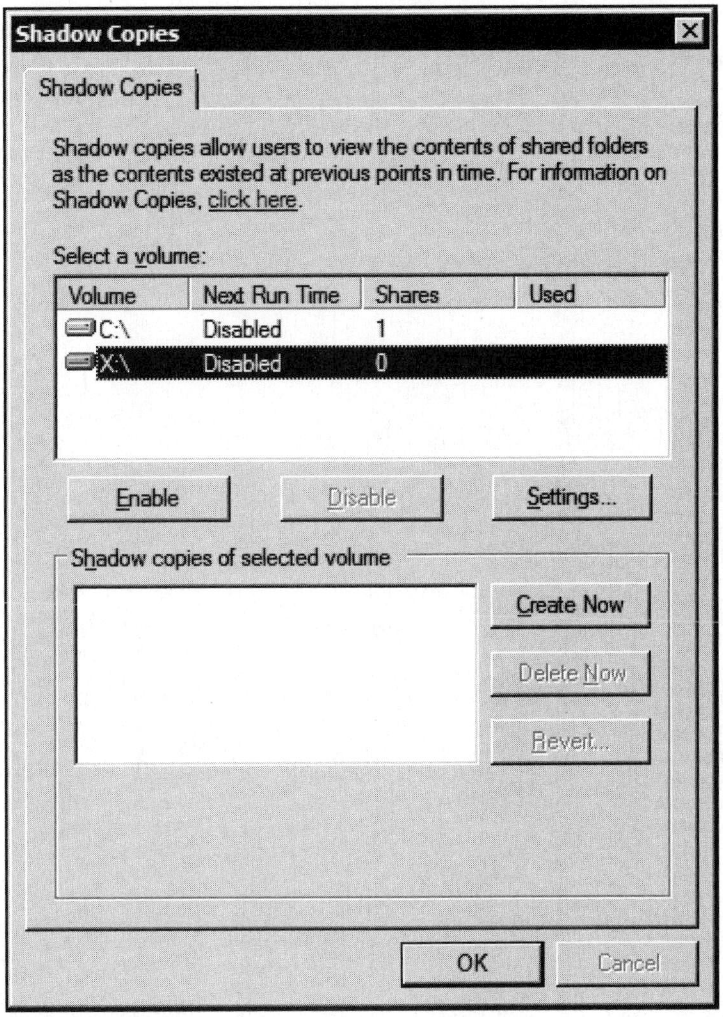

Figure 7-1
Shadow Copies dialog box

2. Select the X:\ volume, and click Enable. An Enable Shadow Copies message box appears, informing you that the selected volume will use the default Shadow Copies settings.

3. Select the Do not show this message again checkbox, and click Yes. The system creates a shadow copy of the selected volume.

4. Click Settings. The Settings dialog box appears.

5. Click Schedule. The X:\ dialog box appears.

6. In the Schedule Task drop-down list, select Daily.

7. Click Advanced. The Advanced Schedule Options dialog box appears.

8. Click the Repeat task checkbox.

9. In the Every spin box, select 5 minutes, and then click OK.

10. Click OK to close the X:\ dialog box.

11. Click OK to close the Settings dialog box, but leave the Shadow Copies dialog box open.

12. In Windows Explorer, browse to the X:\WinSvr2008\sources folder, and double-click a Rich Text Document file named vofflps. A WordPad window appears, displaying the file.

13. At the top of the document, key your first name, and click File > Save.

14. Switch to the Shadow Copies dialog box, and click Create Now.

15. Switch to the WordPad window, key your surname into the document, and click File > Save.

16. Close the WordPad window.

17. Switch to the Shadow Copies dialog box, and click Create Now.

18. Press Ctrl+Prt Scr to take a screen shot of the Shadow Copies dialog box, showing the three shadow copies of the X:\volume you created, and then press Ctrl+V to paste the resulting image into the lab07_worksheet file in the page provided.

19. Close the Shadow Copies dialog box.

20. In Windows Explorer, right-click the vofflps file and, from the context menu, select Properties. The vofflps Properties sheet appears.

21. Click the Previous Versions tab.

Question 1	*Why are there only two previous versions listed when you created three shadow copies with three distinct versions of the vofflps file?*

22. Press Ctrl+Prt Scr to take a screen shot of the vofflps Properties sheet, showing the Previous Versions tab, and then press Ctrl+V to paste the resulting image into the lab07_worksheet file in the page provided.

23. In the vofflps Properties dialog box, select the bottom version listed, and click Open. Another WordPad window appears.

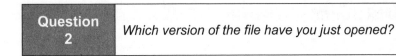

Question 2	Which version of the file have you just opened?

24. Close the WordPad window.

25. Click OK to close the vofflps Properties dialog box.

26. Close the Windows Explorer window.

Exercise 7.3	**Deploying the Web Server (IIS) Role**
Overview	A Network Load Balancing (NLB) cluster enables multiple servers to work together by running the same application and sharing the client load between them. To test NLB, you must first install and configure an application on your server, such as Internet Information Services.
Completion time	15 minutes

1. Click Start, and then click Administrative Tools > Server Manager. Click Continue in the User Account Control message box, and the Server Manager console appears.

2. Select the Roles node and, in the detail pane, click Add Roles. The Add Roles Wizard appears.

3. Click Next to bypass the *Before You Begin* page. The *Select Server Roles* page appears.

4. Select the Web Server (IIS) checkbox, and click Next. An Add Roles Wizard message box appears, listing the features that are required to add the Web Server (IIS) role.

5. Click Add Required Features, and then click Next. The *Introduction to Web Server (IIS)* page appears.

6. Click Next to bypass the introductory page. The *Select Role Services* page appears, as shown in Figure 7-2.

7. Select the Security > Windows Authentication checkbox, and click Next. The *Confirm Installation Selections* page appears.

8. Click Install. The wizard installs the role.

9. Click Close.

10. Close the Server Manager console.

11. Click Start, and then click All Programs > Accessories > Notepad. A Notepad window appears.

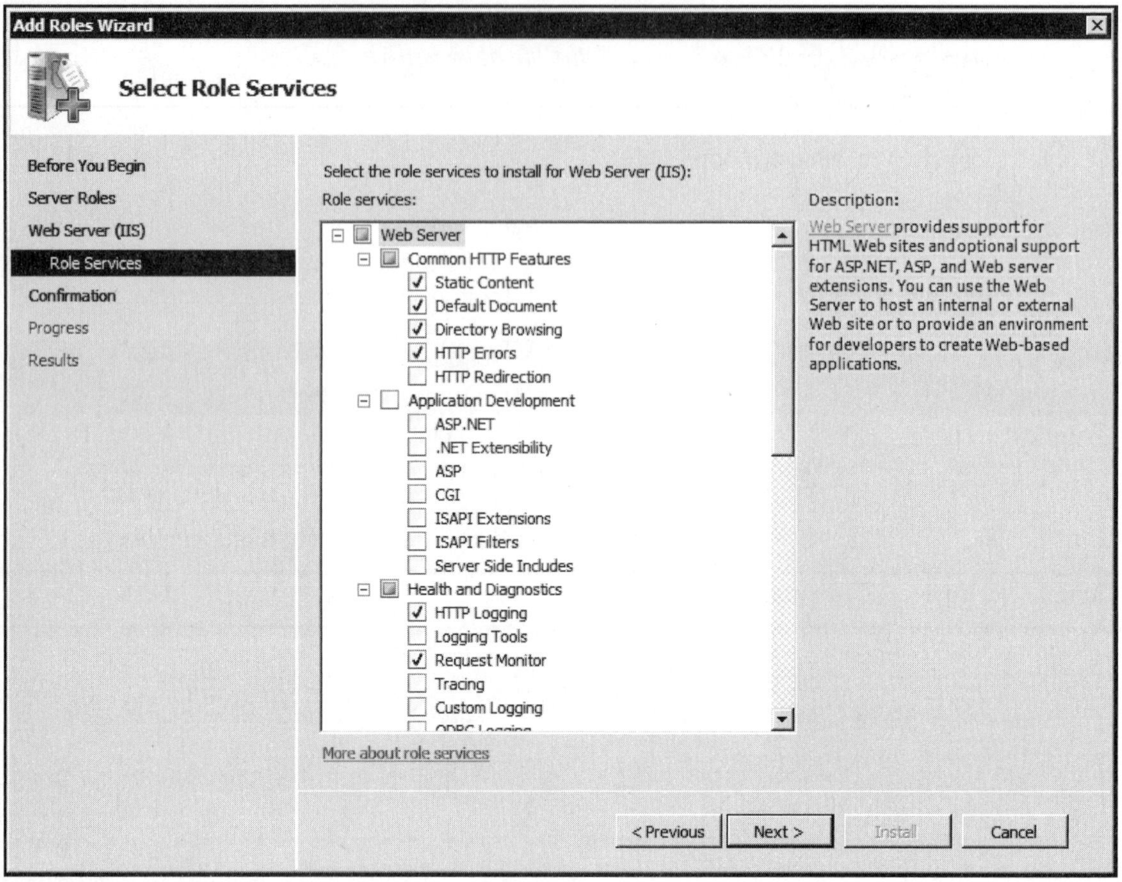

Figure 7-2
Select Role Services page of the Add Roles Wizard

12. In the Notepad window, key the following text, replacing the ## with the number assigned to your server:

```
<html><body>

<h1><center>You have connected to
server##.contoso.com </center></h1>

</html></body>
```

13. Click File > Save As. The Save As dialog box appears.

14. In the Save As Type drop-down list, select All Files.

15. In the File Name text box, key **default.htm**, and click Save.

16. Close the Notepad window.

17. Click Start, and then click Internet Explorer. An Internet Explorer window appears.

18. In the address box, key **http://server##**, where ## is the number assigned to your computer, and press Enter.

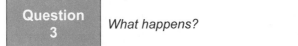

Question 3	*What happens?*

19. Click Start, and then click Administrative Tools > Internet Information Services (IIS) Manager. Click Continue in the User Account Control message box, and the Internet Information Services (IIS) Manager console appears.

20. Expand the SERVER## node and the Sites node, and then select Default Web Site.

21. In the actions pane, click Basic Settings. The Edit Site dialog box appears.

22. In the Physical Path text box, key **\\ServerDC\Students\student##\Documents**, where ## is the number assigned to your computer.

23. Click Connect As. The Connect As dialog box appears.

24. Select the Specific User option, and click Set. The Set Credentials dialog box appears.

25. In the User Name text box, key **contoso\student##**, where ## is the number assigned to your computer.

26. In the Password and Confirm Password text boxes, key **P@ssw0rd**, and click OK.

27. Click OK to close the Connect As dialog box.

28. Click OK to close the Edit Site dialog box.

29. Double-click the Authentication icon. The *Authentication* page appears.

30. Select Windows Authentication and, in the actions pane, click Enable.

31. Close the Internet Information Services (IIS) Manager console.

32. In the Internet Explorer window, click the Refresh button.

Question 4	*What happens?*

33. Press Ctrl+Prt Scr to take a screen shot of the Internet Explorer window, and then press Ctrl+V to paste the resulting image into the lab07_worksheet file in the page provided.

34. Leave the computer logged on for the next exercise.

Exercise 7.4	Installing Network Load Balancing
Overview	To create an NLB cluster, you must install the Network Load Balancing feature using Server Manager.
Completion time	15 minutes

1. Click Start, and then click Administrative Tools > Server Manager. Click Continue in the User Account Control message box, and the Server Manager console appears.

2. Select the Features node and, in the detail pane, click Add Features. The Add Features Wizard appears, displaying the *Select Features* page, as shown in Figure 7-3.

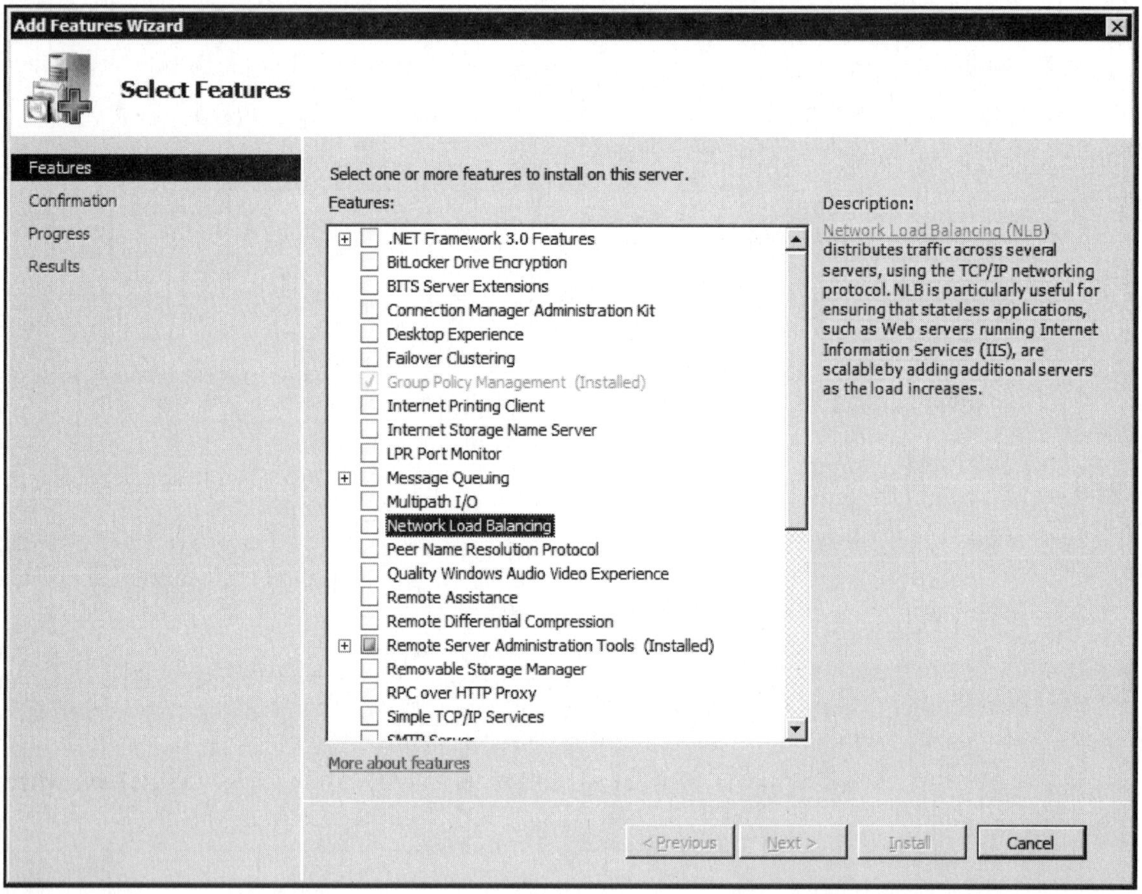

Figure 7-3
Select Features page of the Add Features Wizard

3. Select the Network Load Balancing checkbox, and click Next. The *Confirm Installation Selections* page appears.

4. Click Install. The wizard installs the Network Load Balancing feature.

5. Click Close. The wizard closes.

6. Close the Server Manager console.

7. Click Start, and then click All Programs > Accessories > Command Prompt. A Command Prompt window appears.

8. In the Command Prompt window, key **ipconfig /all**, and press Enter.

9. From the resulting output, fill out the fields in Table 7-1.

Table 7-1
Student Server Configuration Parameters

IP address	
Subnet mask	
Default gateway	
Preferred DNS Server	

10. Close the Command Prompt window.

11. Click Start, and then click Control Panel. The Control Panel window appears.

12. Double-click the Network and Sharing Center icon. The Network and Sharing Center window appears.

13. Click Manage Network Connections. The Network Connections window appears.

14. Right-click the Local Area Connection icon and, from the context menu, select Properties. Click Continue in the User Account Control message box, and the Local Area Connection Properties sheet appears.

15. Select Internet Protocol Version 4 (TCP/IPv4), and click Properties. The Internet Protocol Version 4 (TCP/IPv4) Properties sheet appears.

16. Select Use The Following IP Address. In the IP Address text box, key **10.1.1.##**, where ## is the number assigned to your computer, with no leading zeroes (that is, 10.1.1.9, not 10.1.1.09).

17. Using the information in Table 7-1, fill in the Subnet Mask, Default Gateway, and Preferred DNS Server text boxes, anf then click OK.

18. Click Close to close the Local Area Connection Properties sheet.

19. Close the Network Connections and Network and Sharing Center windows.

20. Leave the computer logged on for the next exercise.

Exercise 7.5   Creating an NLB Cluster

Overview	Creating an NLB cluster enables you to distribute incoming client traffic among multiple servers running an identical application. In this exercise, you create an NLB cluster on your computer to balance traffic for the Web site you created in Exercise 7.4.
Completion time	15 minutes

NOTE	*A Windows Server 2008 network interface can only participate in one NLB cluster at a time. To complete this lab, your server and your partner server must take turns functioning as the primary cluster host and the additional cluster host. After Exercises 7.3 and 7.4 are completed on both servers, you can create, test, and remove a cluster by completing Exercises 7.5, 7.6, 7.7, and 7.8 while your partner server remains idle. After you have removed your cluster, the computers can switch roles so you can complete the same four exercises on your partner server. At no time should the two computers be running two separate clusters.*

1. Click Start, and then click Administrative Tools > Network Load Balancing Manager. Click Continue in the User Account Control message box, and the Network Load Balancing Manager console appears, as shown in Figure 7-4.

2. Right-click the Network Load Balancing Clusters node and, from the context menu, select New Cluster. The New Cluster Wizard appears, displaying the *Connect* page.

3. In the Host text box, key **server##**, where ## is the number assigned to your computer, and click Connect. The wizard connects to your server and displays its network interface.

4. Select the network interface, and click Next. The *Host Parameters* page appears.

5. Click Next to accept the default settings. The *Cluster IP Addresses* page appears.

6. Click Add. The Add IP Address dialog box appears.

7. In the IPv4 Address text box, key **10.1.1.2##**, where ## is the number assigned to your computer.

8. In the Subnet Mask text box, key **255.255.255.0**, and click OK. The address appears in the Cluster IP Addresses box.

9. Click Next. The *Cluster Parameters* page appears.

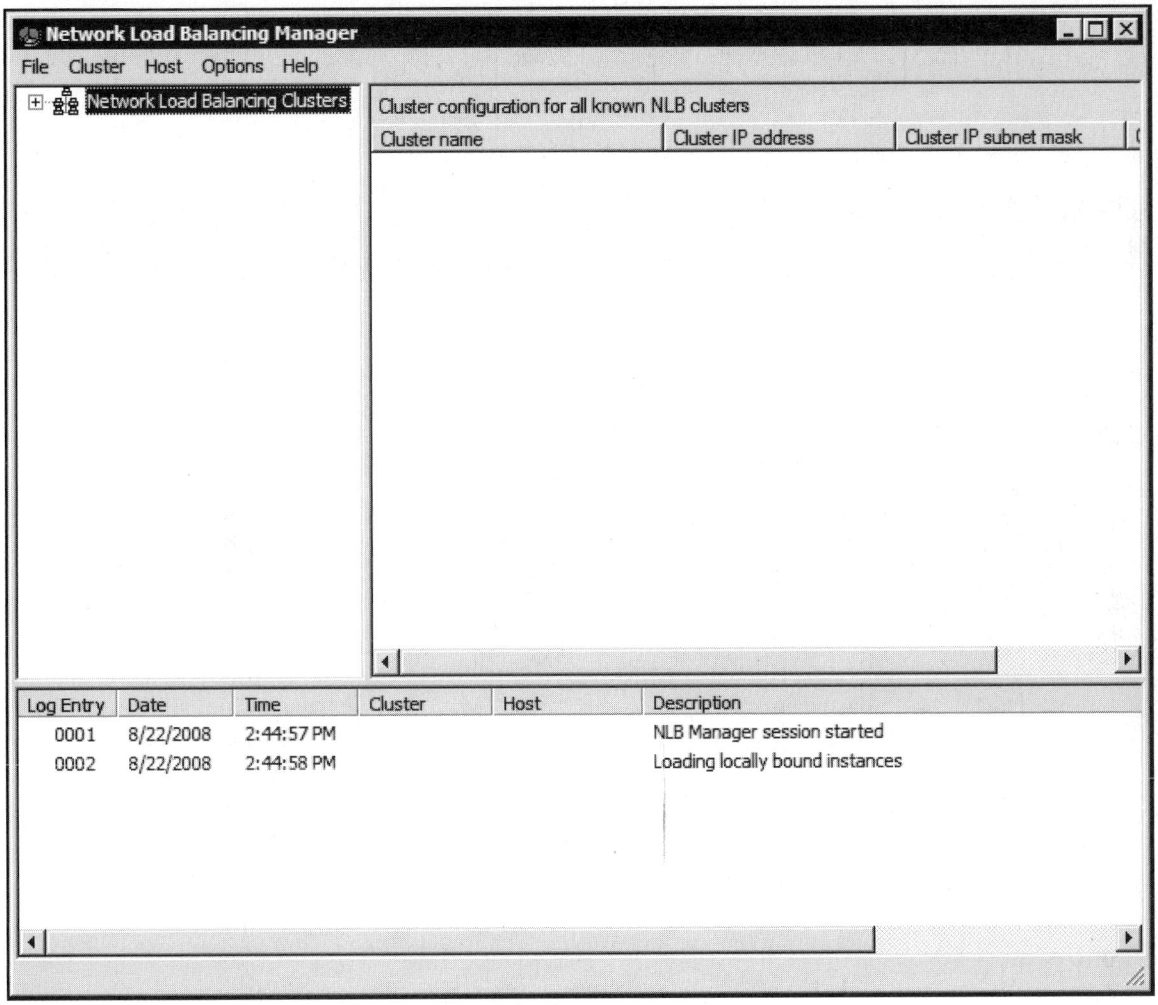

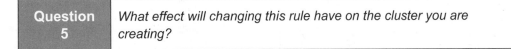

Figure 7-4
Network Load Balancing Manager console

10. In the Full Internet Name text box, key **www##.contoso.com**, where ## is the number assigned to your computer, and then click Next. The *Port Rules* page appears.

11. Select the default rule, and click Edit. The Add/Edit Port Rule dialog box appears.

12. In the Port Range box, set both the From and To spin-boxes to 80, and click OK.

Question 5	*What effect will changing this rule have on the cluster you are creating?*

13. Click Finish. The cluster appears in the Network Load Balancing Manager console.

14. Press Ctrl+Prt Scr to take a screen shot of the Network Load Balancing Manager console, showing the cluster you just created, and then press Ctrl+V to paste the resulting image into the lab07_worksheet file in the page provided.

15. Leave the Network Load Balancing Manager console open for the next exercise.

Exercise 7.6	Adding an NLB Cluster Host
Overview	Once you have created an NLB cluster, you can add and remove hosts at will.
Completion time	10 minutes

> **NOTE**
>
> *Before you begin this exercise, be sure that Exercises 7.3 and 7.4 have been completed on your partner server, in their entirety, and that your partner server is not already hosting an NLB cluster.*

1. In the Network Load Balancing Manager console, right-click the www##.contoso.com cluster you creasted in Exercise 7.5. From the context menu, select Add Host To Cluster. The Add Host To Cluster Wizard appears, displaying the *Connect* page.

2. In the Host text box, key **server##**, where ## is the number assigned to your partner server, and click Connect. The wizard connects to your partner server and displays its network interface.

3. Select the network interface, and click Next. The *Host Parameters* page appears.

4. Click Next to accept the default settings. The *Port Rules* page appears.

5. Click Finish. Your partner server is added to the cluster as a host.

6. Press Ctrl+Prt Scr to take a screen shot of the Network Load Balancing Manager console, showing the cluster with two hosts, and then press Ctrl+V to paste the resulting image into the lab07_worksheet file in the page provided.

7. Close the Network Load Balancing Manager console.

8. Leave the computer logged on for the next exercise.

Exercise 7.7	Testing an NLB Cluster
Overview	In this exercise, you confirm that you are able to connect the cluster and test its fault tolerance.
Completion time	10 minutes

1. Click Start, and then click Internet Explorer. An Internet Explorer window appears.

2. In the address box, key **http://10.1.1.2##**, where ## is the number assigned to your computer, and press Enter.

Question 6	*What happens?*

Question 7	*How do you know that you have connected to the cluster?*

3. In the address box, key **http://www##.contoso.com**, where ## is the number assigned to your computer, and press Enter.

Question 8	*What is the result?*

4. Close all open windows, and shut down your computer.

5. Move to your partner server, and log on using your Student## account and the password *P@ssw0rd*.

6. Click Start, and then click Internet Explorer. An Internet Explorer window appears.

7. In the address box, key **http://10.1.1.2##**, where ## is the number assigned to your computer, and press Enter.

Question 9	*What happens?*

8. On your partner server, click Start, and then click Administrative Tools > Network Load Balancing Manager. Click Continue in the User Account Control message box, and the Network Load Balancing Manager console appears. Bypass any warning messages that appear.

9. If the cluster does not already appear in the console, click Cluster > Connect to Existing. The Connect To Existing Wizard appears, displaying the *Connect* page.

10. In the Host text box, key **server##**, where ## is the number assigned to your partner server, and click Connect. The wizard connects to the server and displays its network interface.

11. Click Finish. The cluster you created on your server appears in the console on your partner server.

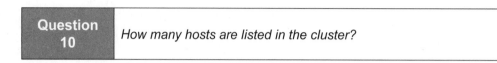

Question 10 | How many hosts are listed in the cluster?

12. Turn on your computer, but do not log on yet.

13. Wait a few minutes, and observe the Network Load Balancing Manager console on your partner server.

Question 11 | What happens?

14. Close the Network Load Balancing Manager console, and log off of your partner server.

Exercise 7.8 Removing an NLB Cluster

Overview	In this exercise, you remove the cluster you created.
Completion time	10 minutes

1. Log on to your computer using your Student## account and the password *P@ssw0rd*.

2. Close the Initial Configuration Tasks window when it appears.

3. Click Start, and then click Administrative Tools > Network Load Balancing Manager. Click Continue in the User Account Control message box, and the Network Load Balancing Manager console appears. Bypass any warning messages that appear.

4. Wait a few minutes until the cluster appears with both hosts.

5. Right-click the www##.contoso.com cluster and, from the context menu, select Delete Cluster. A Network Load Balancing Manager message box appears, confirming that you want to delete the cluster from all of the hosts.

6. Click Yes. The cluster is deleted.

7. Close the Network Load Balancing Manager console, and log off of the computer.

LAB REVIEW QUESTIONS

Completion time	10 minutes

1. In Exercise 7.5, why is it necessary to supply a new IP address for the cluster?

2. In Exercise 7.7, you were able to connect to your NLB cluster using its IP address (10.1.1.2##), but an attemp to connect using its name (www##.contoso.com) failed. Why was this the case?

3. In Exercise 7.7, why was it still possible to connect to the cluster, even though the computer on which you created the cluster was turned off?

LAB CHALLENGE: CREATING A FAILOVER CLUSTER

Completion time	20 minutes

Unlike Network Load Balancing clusters, which are designed to support large amounts of client traffic volume, failover clusters operate as more of a fault tolerance mechanism. To complete this exercise, you must validate and create a two-node failover cluster using your server and your partner server. Give the cluster the name **failover##**, where ## is the number assigned to your computer. List the steps you performed in the process, and save copies of the Failover Cluster Validation report and the Create Cluster report to your Student##\Documents folder on ServerDC. Press Ctrl+Prt Scr to take a screen shot of the Failover Cluster Management console, and then press Ctrl+V to paste the resulting image into the lab07_worksheet file in the page provided.

As with the Network Load Balancing exercises earlier in this lab, you cannot create a failover cluster on both your server and your partner server at the same time. You must create the cluster on your server and then remove it before it is possible to create one on your partner server.

WORKSTATION RESET: RETURNING TO BASELINE

Completion time	10 minutes

To return the computer to its baseline state, complete the following procedures.

1. Open the Network and Sharing Center control panel.

2. Click Manage Network Connections. The Network Connections window appears.

3. Right-click the Local Area Connection icon and, from the context menu, select Properties. Click Continue in the User Account Control message box, and the Local Area Connection Properties sheet appears.

4. Select Internet Protocol Version 4 (TCP/IPv4), and click Properties. The Internet Protocol Version 4 (TCP/IPv4) Properties sheet appears.

5. Select the Obtain An IP Address Automatically option and the Obtain DNS Server Address Automatically option. Click OK, and then click Close.

6. Open Server Manager, and delete the Failover Clustering and Network Load Balancing features.

7. Delete the Web Server (IIS) role.

8. Close all open windows, and log off of the computer.

LAB 8
SECURING A SERVER

This lab contains the following exercises and activities:

Exercise 8.1	Creating Users and User Groups
Exercise 8.2	Creating a Share
Exercise 8.3	Assigning Permissions
Exercise 8.4	Testing Share Access
Lab Review	Questions
Lab Challenge	Configuring Password Policies

BEFORE YOU BEGIN

The classroom network consists of Windows Server 2008 student servers that are all connected to a local area network. There is also a classroom server, named ServerDC, that is connected to the same classroom network. ServerDC is also running Windows Server 2008 and is the domain controller for a domain named contoso.com. Throughout the labs in this manual, you will be working with the same student server on which you will install, configure, maintain, and troubleshoot application roles, features, and services.

Your instructor should have supplied you with the information needed to fill in the following table:

Student computer name (Server##)	
Student account name (Student##)	

To complete the exercises in this lab, you will require access to a second student computer on the classroom network, referred to in the exercises as your *partner server*. Depending on the configuration of your network, use one of the following options as directed by your instructor:

- For a conventional classroom network with one operating system installed on each computer, you must have a lab partner with his or her own computer, performing the same exercises as yourself.

- For a classroom in which each computer uses local virtualization software to install multiple operating systems, you must run two virtual machines representing student computers and perform the exercises separately on each virtual machine.

- For a classroom that uses online virtualization, you will have access to two virtual student servers in your Web browser. You must perform the exercises separately on each virtual machine.

Working with Lab Worksheets

Each lab in this manual requires that you answer questions, shoot screen shots, or perform other activities that you are to document in a worksheet named for the lab, such as lab01_worksheet. Your instructor will supply you with the worksheet files by copying them to the Students\Worksheets share on ServerDC. As you perform the exercises in each lab, open the appropriate worksheet file using WordPad, fill in the required information, and save the file to your computer's Student##\Documents folder. This folder is automatically redirected to the ServerDC computer. Your instructor will examine these worksheet files to assess your performance.

The procedure for opening and saving a worksheet file is as follows:

1. Click Start, and then click Run. The Run dialog box appears.

2. In the Open text box, key **\\ServerDC\Students\Worksheets\lab##_worksheet** (where lab## contains the number of the lab you're completing), and click OK.

3. The worksheet document opens in WordPad.

4. Complete all of the exercises in the worksheet.

5. In WordPad, choose Save As from the File menu. The Save As dialog box appears.

6. In the File Name text box, key **lab##_worksheet_*yourname*** (where lab## contains the number of the lab you're completing and *yourname* is your last name), and click Save.

SCENARIO

The users in your company's Accounting department work with sensitive and confidential information, and your supervisor has instructed you to create a lab network prototype that implements extra security measures for their computers. In this lab, you will create user accounts for the department and use permissions and Group Policy settings to protect their computers and their data.

After completing this lab, you will be able to:

■   Create users and groups

■   Create shares

■   Assign NTFS and share permissions

■   Configure password policies

Estimated lab time: 90 minutes

Exercise 8.1	Creating Users and User Groups
Overview	In this exercise, you create the user accounts for the Accounting department staff as well as the groups that you will use to provide them with the permissions they need.
Completion time	15 minutes

1.   Turn on your computer. When the logon screen appears, log on using your Student## account and the password *P@ssw0rd*.

2.   Close the Initial Configuration Tasks window when it appears.

3.   Click Start, and then click Administrative Tools > Active Directory Users and Computers. Click Continue in the User Account Control message box, and the Active Directory Users and Computers console appears.

4.   Expand the contoso.com node.

5.   Right-click the contoso.com node and, from the context menu, select New > Organizational Unit. The New Object - Organizational Unit dialog box appears.

6.   In the Name text box, key **Accounting##**, where ## is the number assigned to your computer, and click OK. The new organizational unit object appears in the contoso.com domain.

7.   Right-click the Accounting## OU you created and, from the context menu, select New > User. The New Object - User Wizard appears, as shown in Figure 8-1.

8.   In the First name text box, key **Karen**.

9.   In the Last name text box, key **Archer**.

10.   In the User logon name text box, key **KarenA##**, where ## is the number assigned to your computer, and click Next.

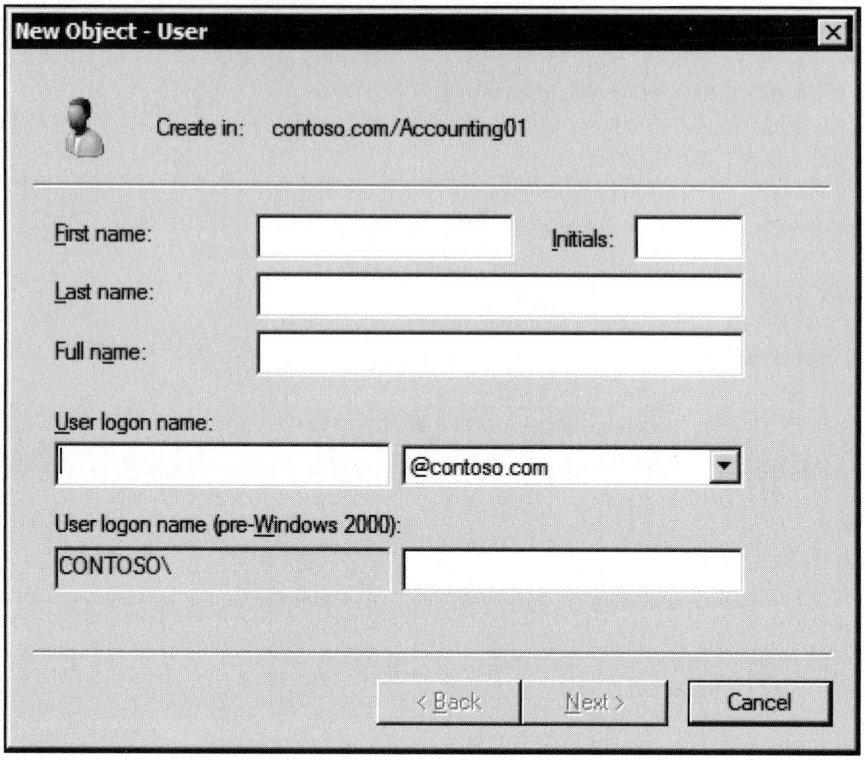

Figure 8-1
New Object - User Wizard

11. In the Password and Confirm Password text boxes, key **P@ssw0rd**.

12. Clear the User Must Change Password At Next Logon checkbox, and click Next.

13. Click Finish. The new user object appears in the Accounting## OU.

14. Repeat steps 7 to 13 to create user objects for the individuals listed in Table 8-1.

15. Right-click the Accounting## OU and, from the context menu, select New > Group. The New Object - Group dialog box appears.

Table 8-1
Accounting Department Users

First Name	Last Name	User Logon Name	Password
Brian	Cox	BrianC##	P@ssw0rd
Mary	Gibson	MaryG##	P@ssw0rd
Ashvini	Sharma	AshviniS##	P@ssw0rd
Marie	Reinhart	MarieR##	P@ssw0rd
Leo	Giakoumakis	LeoG##	P@ssw0rd

16. In the Group Name text box, key **Acctg##-Users**, and click OK. The group appears in the Accounting## OU.

17. Repeat steps 15 to 16 to create two additional groups named **Acctg##-Managers** and **Acctg##-Interns**.

18. Double-click the Acctg##-Users group. The Acctg##-Users Properties sheet appears.

19. Click the Members tab.

20. Click Add. The Select Users, Contacts, Computers, or Groups dialog box appears.

21. In the Enter The Object Names To Select box, key **Karen Archer**; **Brian Cox**; **Mary Gibson**; **Ashvini Sharma**; **Marie Reinhart**, and click OK. The users appear in the Members list.

22. Repeat steps 18 to 21 to make Karen Archer and Brian Cox members of the Acctg##-Managers group.

23. Repeat steps 18 to 21 to make Leo Giakoumakis a member of the Acctg##-Interns group.

24. Press Ctrl+Prt Scr to take a screen shot of the Active Directory Users and Computers console, showing the Accounting## OU and the objects you created in it, and then press Ctrl+V to paste the resulting image into the lab08_worksheet file in the page provided.

25. Close the Active Directory Users and Computers console.

26. Leave the computer logged on for the next exercise.

Exercise 8.2	**Creating a Share**
Overview	In this exercise, you create the network share where the Accounting department will store its confidential files.
Completion time	10 minutes

1. Click Start, and then click Administrative Tools > Server Manager. Click Continue in the User Account Control message box, and the Server Manager console appears.

Question 1	*According to the Server Manager console, what roles are currently installed on the computer?*

2. Click Start, and then click Administrative Tools > Share and Storage Management. Click Continue in the User Account Control message box, and the Share and Storage Management console appears, as shown in Figure 8-2.

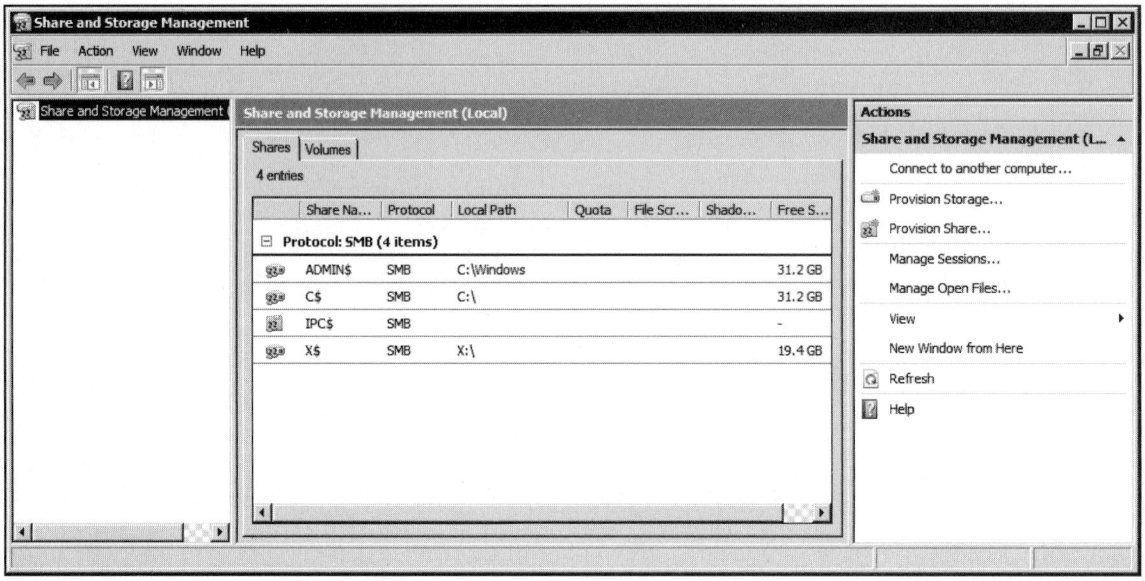

Figure 8-2
Share and Storage Management console

3. In the detail (middle) pane, click the Volumes tab.

> **NOTE**
> *If the Data (X:) volume does not appear in the Volumes list, return to Lab 7, "Using High-Availability Features," and complete Exercise 7.1 before you continue.*

4. In the actions pane, click Provision Share. The Provision a Shared Folder Wizard appears, displaying the *Shared Folder Location* page.

5. Click Browse. The Browse For Folder dialog box appears.

6. Select x$, and click Make New Folder.

7. Key **Budget**, and click OK. The X:\Budget folder appears in the Location text box.

8. Click Next. The *NTFS Permissions* page appears.

9. Click Next to accept the default setting. The *Share Protocols* page appears.

Question 2	*Why is the NFS option grayed out on the Share Protocols page?*

10.   Click Next to accept the default SMB share name. The *SMB Settings* page appears.

11.   Click Next to accept the default settings. The *SMB Permissions* page appears.

12.   Select Administrators Have Full Control; All Other Users And Groups Have Only Read Access, and click Next. The *DFS Namespace Publishing* page appears.

13.   Click Next. The *Review Settings and Create Share* page appears.

14.   Click Create. The wizard creates the share, and the *Confirmation* page appears.

15.   Click Close. The Budget share appears in the console on the Shares tab.

16.   Press Ctrl+Prt Scr to take a screen shot of the Share and Storage Management console, showing the share you just created, and then press Ctrl+V to paste the resulting image into the lab08_worksheet file in the page provided.

17.   Wait two minutes, and switch back to the Server Manager console.

	What installed roles appear in the Server Manager console now? Why has there been a change?

18.   Close the Server Manager console and the Share and Storage Management console.

19.   Leave the computer logged on for the next exercise.

Exercise 8.3	**Assigning Permissions**
Overview	In this exercise, you create domain local groups and assign the NTFS permissions that will grant the groups access to the folders on the network share.
Completion time	20 minutes

1.   Click Start, and then click Administrative Tools > Active Directory Users and Computers. Click Continue in the User Account Control message box, and the Active Directory Users and Computers console appears.

2.   Expand the contoso.com node.

3.   Right-click the Accounting## OU and, from the context menu, select New > Group. The New Object - Group dialog box appears.

4.   In the Group Name text box, key **Budget##-Full**, where ## is the number assigned to your computer.

5. In the Group Scope box, select Domain Local, and click OK. The group appears in the Accounting## OU.

6. Repeat steps 3 to 5 to create two more domain local groups named **Budget##-RW** and **Budget##-RO**.

7. Click Start, and then click All Programs > Accessories > Windows Explorer. A Windows Explorer window appears.

8. Browse to the Budget folder on the X: drive, right-click the Budget folder and, from the context menu, select Properties. The Budget Properties sheet appears.

9. Click the Security tab, as shown in Figure 8-3.

10. Click Edit. Click Continue in the User Account Control message box, and the Permissions for Budget dialog box appears.

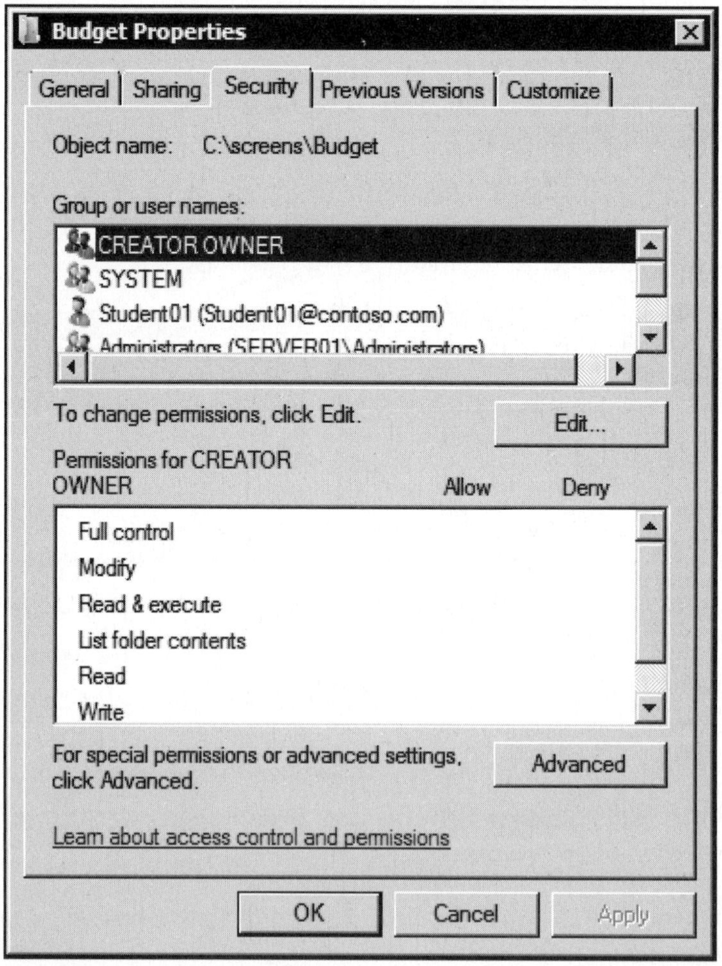

Figure 8-3
Security tab of the Budget folder

11. Click Add. The Select Users, Computers, or Groups dialog box appears.

12. In the Enter The Object Names To Select text box, key **Budget##-Full**; **Budget##-RW**; **Budget##-RO**, and click OK. The three groups appear in the Group or User Names list.

13. Select the Budget##-Full group and, in the Permissions for Budget##-Full box, select the Allow Full Control permission.

14. Select the Budget##-RO group, and, in the Permissions for Budget##-RO box, make sure that only the Allow Read & Execute, Allow List Folder Contents, and Allow Read permissions are selected.

15. Select the Budget##-RW group and, in the Permissions for Budget##-RW box, select the Allow Write and Allow Modify permissions.

16. Click OK to close the Permissions for Budget dialog box.

17. Press Ctrl+Prt Scr to take a screen shot of the Budget Properties sheet, showing the Security tab and the three security principals you just added, and then press Ctrl+V to paste the resulting image into the lab08_worksheet file in the page provided.

18. Click OK to close the Budget Properties sheet.

19. Click Start, and then click Administrative Tools > Active Directory Users and Computers. Click Continue in the User Account Control message box, and the Active Directory Users and Computers console appears.

20. Expand the contoso.com node, and select your Accounting## OU.

21. Double-click the Budget##-Full group. The Budget##-Full Properties sheet appears.

22. Click the Members tab.

23. Click Add. The Select Users, Contacts, Computers, or Groups dialog box appears.

24. In the Enter The Object Names To Select box, key **Acctg##-Managers**, and click OK. The group appears in the Members list.

25. Click OK to close the Budget##-Full Properties sheet.

26. Repeat steps 21 to 25 to make the Acctg##-Users group a member of the Budget##-RW group.

27. Repeat steps 21 to 25 to make the Acctg##-Interns group a member of the Budget##-RO group.

28. Close the Active Directory Users and Computers console.

29. Log off of the computer.

Exercise 8.4	Testing Share Access
Overview	In this exercise, you test the permissions you created by logging on using the accounts you created in Exercise 8.1.
Completion time	15 minutes

1. On your server, log on to the contoso.com domain using the KarenA## account you created and the password *P@ssw0rd*.

2. Click Start, and then click All Programs > Accessories > Windows Explorer. A Windows Explorer window appears.

3. Browse to the Budget folder on the X: drive, right-click in the view pane and, from the context menu, select New > Rich Text Document. A new document appears.

4. Key **Report##**, where ## is the number assigned to your computer, and press Enter to name the file.

5. Double-click the Report## file. A WordPad window appears.

6. Key some text in the document, and click File > Save.

7. Close the WordPad window, and log off of the computer.

8. Move to your partner server, and log on to the contoso.com domain using the LeoG## account you created and the password *P@ssw0rd*.

9. Click Start, and then click Run. The Run dialog box appears.

10. In the Open text box, key **\\server##\budget**, and click OK. A Windows Explorer window appears.

11. Double-click the Report## file. A WordPad window appears.

12. Modify the text in the file, and click File > Save. A message box appears, indicating that access to the file has been denied.

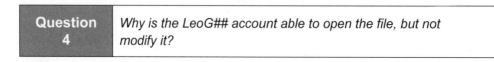

Question 4	*Why is the LeoG## account able to open the file, but not modify it?*

13. Log off of your partner server.

14. While still on your partner server, log on to the contoso.com domain using the MarieR## account you created and the password *P@ssw0rd*.

15. Repeat steps 9 to 12 to try to modify the Report## file.

Question 5	*What is the result?*

16. Log off of the computer, and log on to the contoso.com domain again using the Karen## account and the password *P@ssw0rd*.

17. Repeat steps 9 to 12 to try to modify the Report## file.

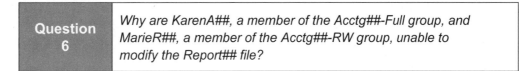

Question 6	*Why are KarenA##, a member of the Acctg##-Full group, and MarieR##, a member of the Acctg##-RW group, unable to modify the Report## file?*

18. On your worksheet, list the steps you must perform to correct the problem and enable the members of the Acctg##-Full and Acctg##-RW groups to modify the Report## file.

19. Close all open windows, and log off of your partner server.

LAB REVIEW QUESTIONS

Completion time   10 minutes

1. In Exercise 8.3, what would happen if you accidentally reversed the group memberships and tried to add the Budget##-Full group as a member of the Acctg##-Full group?

2. If Leo Giakoumakis is hired as a full-time employee after his internship ends, what would you have to do to grant him the permissions to the Budget share that he needs?

3. In Exercise 8.4, what test could you perform to prove that your reason for KarenA##'s and MarieR##'s inability to modify the Report## file is correct?

LAB CHALLENGE: CONFIGURING PASSWORD POLICIES

Completion time   20 minutes

The IT director is planning to deploy the Accounting department network as a separate domain, and she wants to impose more stringent password and account requirements on them. To complete this exercise, you must create a new Group Policy object in the contoso.com domain named Accounting##, where ## is the number assigned to your computer, that enforces the following policies:

- Users must change their passwords weekly.

- Users can reuse any password for a period of four months.

- User passwords must be ten characters or longer and include a combination of uppercase letters, lowercase letters, and numbers.

- Users have three chances to log on correctly during a one-hour period, after which the account is locked until an administrator releases it.

Do not link the Group Policy object to an Active Directory object. Simply create the GPO. List the steps you performed in this process. Press Ctrl+Prt Scr to take screen shots of the Group Policy Management Editor console, showing the policy settings you configured, and then press Ctrl+V to paste the resulting image into the lab08_worksheet file in the page provided.

No workstation reset is necessary before beginning the next lab.

LAB 9
SECURING INFRASTRUCTURE SERVICES

This lab contains the following exercises and activities:

BEFORE YOU BEGIN

The classroom network consists of Windows Server 2008 student servers that are all connected to a local area network. There is also a classroom server, named ServerDC, that is

connected to the same classroom network. ServerDC is also running Windows Server 2008 and is the domain controller for a domain named contoso.com. Throughout the labs in this manual, you will be working with the same student server on which you will install, configure, maintain, and troubleshoot application roles, features, and services.

Your instructor should have supplied you with the information needed to fill in the following table:

Student computer name (Server ##)	
Student account name (Student ##)	

To complete the exercises in this lab, you will require access to a second student computer on the classroom network, referred to in the exercises as your *partner server*. Depending on the configuration of your network, use one of the following options as directed by your instructor:

- For a conventional classroom network with one operating system installed on each computer, you must have a lab partner with his or her own computer, performing the same exercises as yourself.

- For a classroom in which each computer uses local virtualization software to install multiple operating systems, you must run two virtual machines representing student computers and perform the exercises separately on each virtual machine.

- For a classroom that uses online virtualization, you will have access to two virtual student servers in your Web browser. You must perform the exercises separately on each virtual machine.

Working with Lab Worksheets

Each lab in this manual requires that you answer questions, shoot screen shots, or perform other activities that you are to document in a worksheet named for the lab, such as lab01_worksheet. Your instructor will supply you with the worksheet files by copying them to the Students\Worksheets share on ServerDC. As you perform the exercises in each lab, open the appropriate worksheet file using WordPad, fill in the required information, and save the file to your computer's Student##\Documents folder. This folder is automatically redirected to the ServerDC computer. Your instructor will examine these worksheet files to assess your performance.

The procedure for opening and saving a worksheet file is as follows:

1. Click Start, and then click Run. The Run dialog box appears.

2. In the Open text box, key **\\ServerDC\Students\Worksheets\lab##_worksheet** (where lab## contains the number of the lab you're completing), and click OK.

3. The worksheet document opens in WordPad.

4. Complete all of the exercises in the worksheet.

5. In WordPad, choose Save As from the File menu. The Save As dialog box appears.

6. In the File Name text box, key **lab##_worksheet_*yourname*** (where lab## contains the number of the lab you're completing and *yourname* is your last name), and click Save.

SCENARIO

Some of your company's branch offices have Accounting department personnel who need to access network resources at the company headquarters. Rather than install costly leased lines, the IT director has decided to install a virtual private network (VPN) server using Windows Server 2008. The directory also wants to explore the possibility of installing a certification authority and issuing certificates to users at remote locations for security purposes. Your task is to implement these technologies in the lab and examine their security capabilities.

After completing this lab, you will be able to:

- Configure Windows Server 2008 to function as a VPN server

- Configure the Windows Server 2008 network connection client to connect to a VPN server

- Install a certification authority

- Create and process certificate enrollment requests

Estimated lab time: 120 minutes

Exercise 9.1	Installing Network Policy and Access Services
Overview	In this exercise, you install the role that implements the Routing and Remote Access service, which enables the server to receive VPN connections from clients on the Internet.
Completion time	5 minutes

1. Turn on your computer. When the logon screen appears, log on to the domain with your Student## account, where ## is the number assigned by your instructor, using the password *P@ssw0rd*.

2. Click Start, and then click Administrative Tools > Server Manager. Click Continue in the User Account Control message box, and the Server Manager console appears.

3. Select the Roles node, and click Add Roles. The Add Roles Wizard appears, displaying the *Before You Begin* page.

4. Click Next to continue. The *Select Server Roles* page appears.

5. Select the Network Policy and Access Services role, and click Next. The *Introduction to Network Policy and Access Services* page appears.

6. Click Next to continue. The *Select Role Services* page appears, as shown in Figure 9-1.

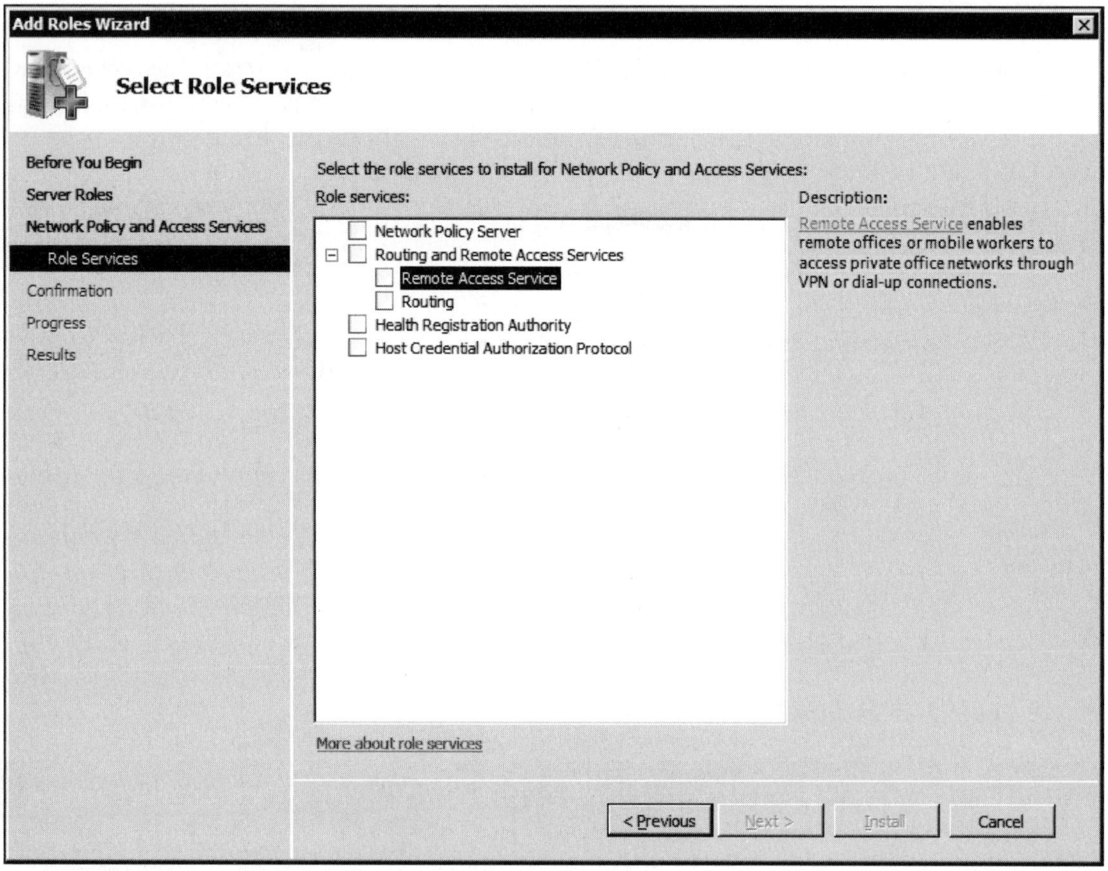

Figure 9-1
Select Role Services page of the Add Roles Wizard

7. Select the Remote Access Service checkbox, and click Next. The *Confirm Installation Selections* page appears.

8. Click Install. The wizard installs the role, and the *Installation Results* page appears.

9. Click Close. The wizard closes.

10. Close the Server Manager console.

11. Leave the computer logged on for the next exercise.

Exercise 9.2	Configuring Routing and Remote Access
Overview	Routing and Remote Access can perform a variety of services In this exercise, you configure the service to function as a VPN server.
Completion time	10 minutes

1. Click Start, and then click Administrative Tools > Routing and Remote Access. Click Continue in the User Account Control message box, and the Routing and Remote Access console appears, as shown in Figure 9-2.

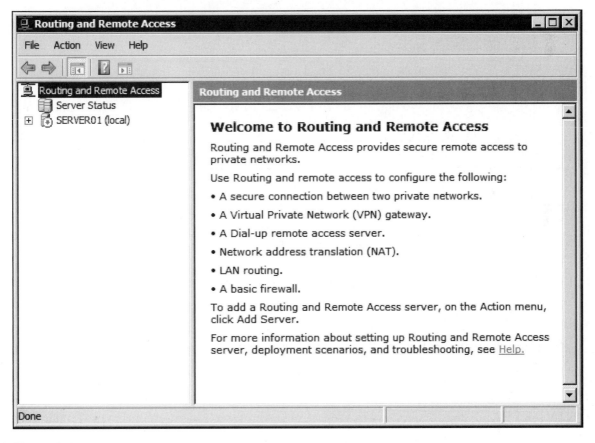

Figure 9-2
Routing and Remote Access console

2. Right-click the SERVER## (local) node and, from the context menu, select Configure and Enable Routing and Remote Access. The Routing and Remote Access Server Setup Wizard appears, displaying the Welcome page.

3. Click Next. The *Configuration* page appears.

4. Select Custom configuration, and click Next. The *Custom Configuration* page appears.

5. Select VPN access, and click Next. The *Completing the Routing and Remote Access Server Setup Wizard* page appears.

6. Click Finish. The Start the service message box appears.

7. Click Start service. The wizard configures the service and closes.

8. Press Ctrl+Prt Scr to take a screen shot of the Routing and Remote Access console, and then press Ctrl+V to paste the resulting image into the lab09_worksheet file in the page provided.

9. Leave the Routing and Remote Access console open for the next exercise.

Exercise 9.3	Configuring a VPN Client
Overview	At this point, both your server and your partner server should be configured to function as VPN servers. In this exercise, you configure Windows Server 2008 to function as a VPN client so you can establish a connection to your partner server.
Completion time	10 minutes

1. Click Start, and then click All Programs > Accessories > Command Prompt. A Command Prompt window appears.

2. At the command prompt, key **ipconfig /all**, and press Enter.

3. Using the information displayed by the ipconfig program, fill out the Your server row in Table 9-1.

Table 9-1
Student server names and addresses

	Computer Name	IPv4 Address
Your server		
Your partner server		

4. Repeat steps 1 to 3 on your partner server, and fill out the Your partner server row in Table 9-1.

5. Click Start, and then click Control Panel. The Control Panel window appears.

6. Double-click the Network and Sharing Center icon. The Network and Sharing Center window appears.

7. Click Connect to a network. The Connect to a network Wizard appears, displaying the *This computer is connected to contoso.com* page.

8. Click Set up a connection or network. The *Choose a connection option* page appears, as shown in Figure 9-3.

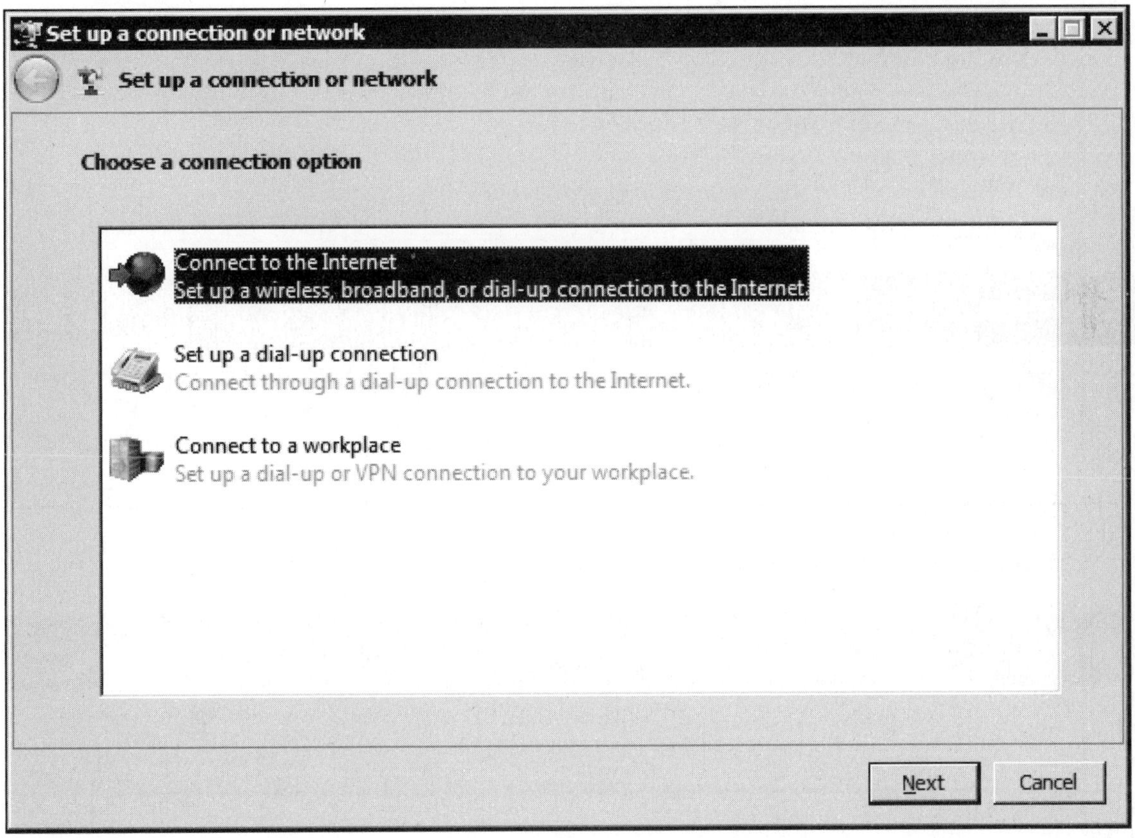

Figure 9-3
Choose a connection option page of the Connect to a network Wizard

9. Select Connect to a workplace, and click Next. The *How do you want to connect?* page appears.

10. Click Use my Internet connection (VPN). The *Do you want to set up an Internet connection before proceeding?* page appears.

11. Click I'll set up an Internet connection later. The *Type the Internet address to connect to* page appears.

12. In the Internet address text box, key the IPv4 address of your partner server from Table 9-1.

13. In the Destination name text box, key **Server ## VPN Connection**.

14. Select the Allow other people to use this connection checkbox, and click Continue in the User Account Control message box.

15. Click Next. The *Type your user name and password* page appears.

16. In the User name text box, key **Student##**, where ## is the number assigned to your computer.

17. In the Password text box, key **P@ssw0rd**.

18. In the Domain text box, key **contoso**.

19. Click Create. The *The connection is ready to use* page appears.

> **NOTE**
>
> *The* The connection is ready to use *page states that you must set up an Internet connection before you can connect to the VPN server. For the purposes of this lab, however, you will be connecting directly to your partner server over the local area network, and no Internet connection is required.*

20. Click Close. The wizard closes.

21. Leave the computer logged on for the next exercise.

Exercise 9.4   Establishing a Connection

Overview	In this exercise, you use the client on your server to establish a VPN connection with your partner server.
Completion time	15 minutes

> **NOTE**
>
> *Before you begin this exercise, make sure that Exercises 9.1 and 9.2 are completed on your partner server. Also, the clients on your server and your partner server must take turns establishing connections. Connecting each client to the other server simultaneously can result in unstable connections.*

1. On the Network and Sharing Center control panel, click Connect to a network. The *Select a network to connect to* page appears.

2. Select Server## VPN Connection, and click Connect. A Connect Server## VPN Connection dialog box appears, as shown in Figure 9-4.

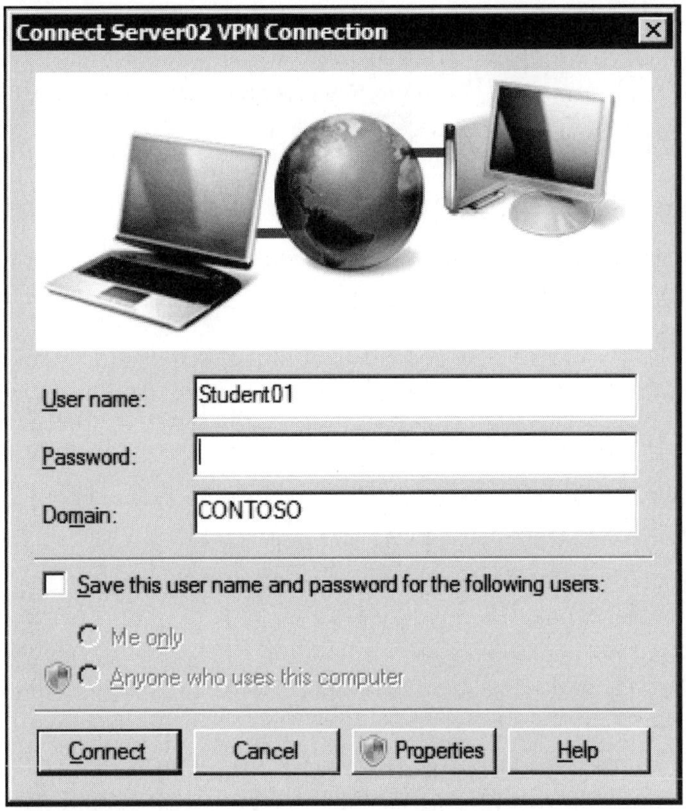

Figure 9-4
Connect Server## VPN Connection dialog box

3. Key in the required credentials using your Student## account name, the password *P@ssw0rd*, and the contoso domain name. Then, click Connect.

Question 1	What happens?

4. Press Ctrl+Prt Scr to take a screen shot of the resulting page, and then press Ctrl+V to paste the resulting image into the lab09_worksheet file in the page provided.

5. Click Cancel. The wizard closes.

6. Click Start, and then click Administrative Tools > Active Directory Users and Computers. Click Continue in the User Account Control message box, and the Active Directory Users and Computers console appears.

7. Expand the contoso.com node, and select the Users container.

8. Double-click the Student## user object, where ## is the number assigned to your computer. The Student## Properties sheet appears.

9. Click the Dial-in tab.

10. In the Network Access Permission box, select Allow Access, and click OK.

11. Repeat steps 1 to 3 to try connecting to your partner server again.

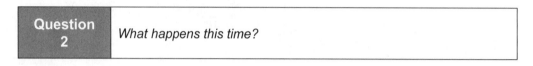

| Question 2 | *What happens this time?* |

12. Press Ctrl+Prt Scr to take a screen shot of the Connect to a network Wizard, showing the results of the connection attempt, and then press Ctrl+V to paste the resulting image into the lab09_worksheet file in the page provided.

13. When your partner server successfully connects to your server, switch to the Routing and Remote Access console.

14. Select the Remote Access Clients node and, if necessary, press the F5 key to refresh the display.

15. Double-click the client connection from your partner server. A Status dialog box appears.

16. Press Ctrl+Prt Scr to take a screen shot of the Status dialog box, and then press Ctrl+V to paste the resulting image into the lab09_worksheet file in the page provided.

17. In the Active Directory Users and Computers console, open the Properties sheet for your Student## user object. On the Dial-In tab, select Control access through NPS Network Policy, and click OK.

18. Close the Active Directory Users and Computers console.

19. Close the Routing and Remote Access console.

20. In the Network and Sharing Center control panel, click Manage Network Connections. The Network Connections window appears.

21. Select the Server## VPN Connection, and click Disconnect this connection.

22. Close the Network Connections window.

23. Close the Network and Sharing Center control panel.

24. Leave the computer logged on for the next exercise.

Exercise 9.5   Installing Active Directory Certificate Services

Overview	The company's branch offices run their own Active Directory domains in separate forests, so the certification authority you install must be independent of the Active Directory infrastructure. In this exercise, you install the Active Directory Certificate Services role and configure it to issue certificates.
Completion time	10 minutes

1. Click Start, and then click Administrative Tools > Server Manager. Click Continue in the User Account Control message box, and the Server Manager console appears.

2. Select the Roles node, and click Add Roles. The Add Roles Wizard appears, displaying the *Before You Begin* page.

3. Click Next to continue. The *Select Server Roles* page appears.

4. Select the Active Directory Certificate Services role, and click Next. The *Introduction to Active Directory Certificate Services* page appears.

5. Click Next to continue. The *Select Role Services* page appears, as shown in Figure 9-5.

6. Select the Certification Authority and Certification Authority Web Enrollment checkboxes. The Add role services required for Certification Authority Web Enrollment dialog box appears.

7. Click Add Required Role Services, and then click Next. The *Specify Setup Type* page appears.

8. Select the Standalone option, and click Next. The *Specify CA Type* page appears.

9. Select the Root CA option, and click Next. The *Set Up Private Key* page appears.

Question 3	*Why can't you select the Subordinate CA option at this time?*

10. Leave the Create a new private key option selected, and click Next. The *Configure Cryptography for CA* page appears.

11. In the Key character length drop-down list, select 4096, and click Next. The *Configure CA Name* page appears.

12. Click Next to accept the default CA name. The *Set Validity Period* page appears.

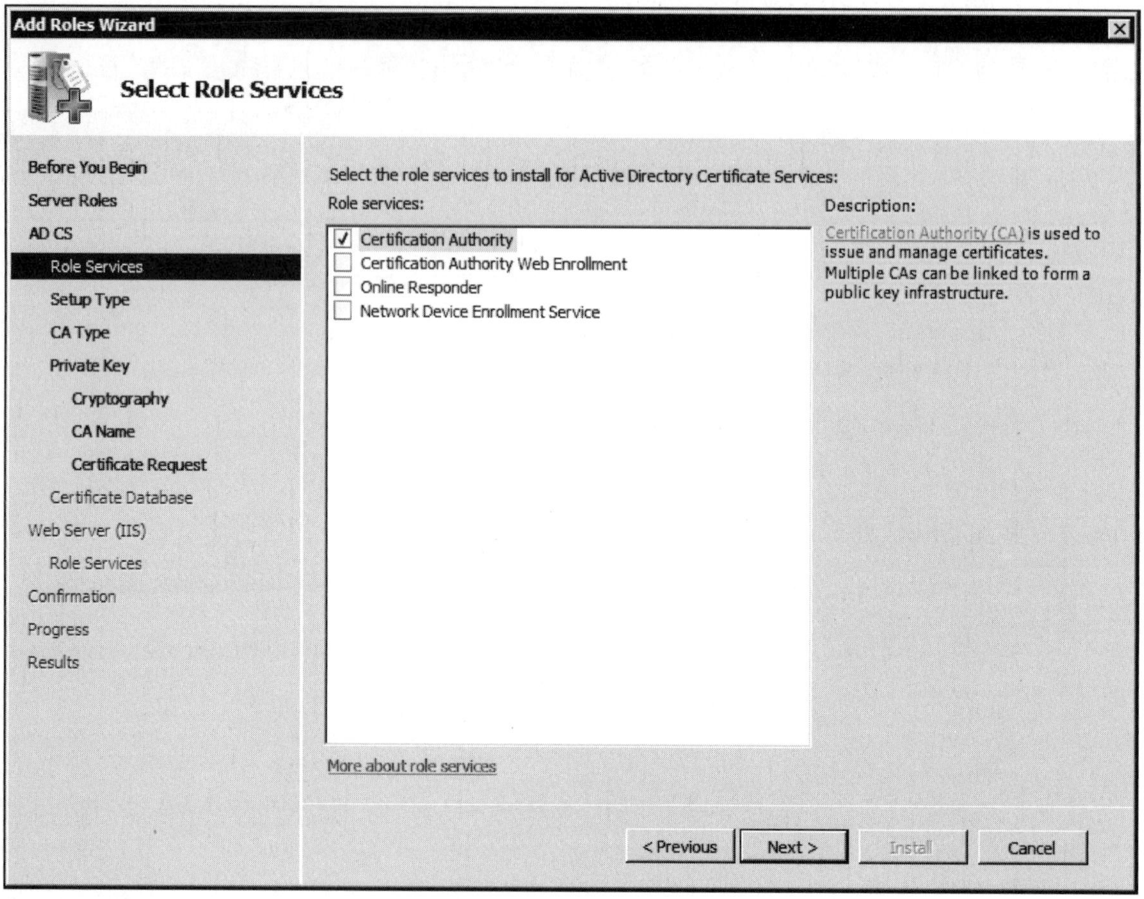

Figure 9-5
Select Role Services page of the Add Roles Wizard

13. Click Next to accept the default 5-year validity period. The *Configure Certificate Database* page appears.

14. Click Next to accept the default database locations. The *Introduction to Web Server (IIS)* page appears.

15. Click Next. The *Select Role Services* page appears.

16. Click Next to accept the default role services. The *Confirm Installation Selections* page appears.

17. Click Install. The wizard installs the roles, and the *Installation Results* page appears.

18. Press Ctrl+Prt Scr to take a screen shot of the *Installation Results* page, and then press Ctrl+V to paste the resulting image into the lab09_worksheet file in the page provided.

19. Click Close. The wizard closes.

20. Close the Server Manager console.

21. Leave the computer logged on for the next exercise.

Exercise 9.6	Using the Certificates Snap-In
Overview	In this exercise, you test the functionality of your certification authority by requesting a certificate using the Certificates snap-in for Microsoft Management Console.
Completion time	10 minutes

1. Click Start, and then click Run. The Run dialog box appears.

2. In the Open text box, key **mmc**, and click OK. Click Continue in the User Account Control message box, and a blank Microsoft Management Console window appears.

3. Click File > Add/Remove Snap-In. The Add or Remove Snap-ins dialog box appears.

4. In the Available snap-ins list, select Certificates, and click Add. The Certificates snap-in dialog box appears.

5. Leave the My user account option selected, and click Finish.

6. Click OK to close the Add or Remove Snap-ins dialog box. The Certificates snap-in appears in the MMC console.

7. Expand the Certificates - Current User node, as shown in Figure 9-6.

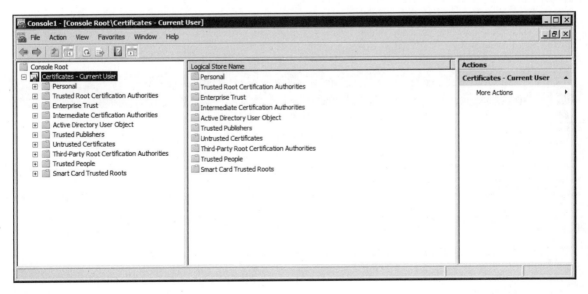

Figure 9-6
Certificates - Current User console

8. Expand the Trusted Root Certification Authorities folder, and select the Certificates folder beneath it.

9. In the list of certificates, locate one named contoso-SERVER##-CA, where ## is the number assigned to your computer, and double-click it. A Certificate dialog box appears.

Question 4	What CA issues this certificate?

10. Press Ctrl+Prt Scr to take a screen shot of the Certificate dialog box, and then press Ctrl+V to paste the resulting image into the lab09_worksheet file in the page provided.

11. Click OK to close the Certificate dialog box.

12. Right-click the Personal folder and, from the context menu, select All Tasks > Request New Certificate. The Certificate Enrollment Wizard appears, displaying the *Before You Begin* page.

13. Click Next. The *Request Certificates* page appears.

14. Select the User checkbox, and click Enroll. The *Requesting certificates* page appears.

15. Press Ctrl+Prt Scr to take a screen shot of the *Failed to install one or more certificates* page, and then press Ctrl+V to paste the resulting image into the lab09_worksheet file in the page provided.

16. Click Close.

17. Close the Certificates console.

18. Leave the computer logged on for the next exercise.

Exercise 9.7	Using Web-Based Enrollment
Overview	In this exercise, you use your CA's Web-based enrollment feature to manually request a certificate, just as your company's remote users will have to do in the future.
Completion time	10 minutes

1. Click Start, and then click Internet Explorer. An Internet Explorer window appears.

2. In the address box, key **http://server##/certsrv**, where ## is the number assigned to your server, and press Enter. *The Microsoft Active Directory Certificate Services* page appears, as shown in Figure 9-7.

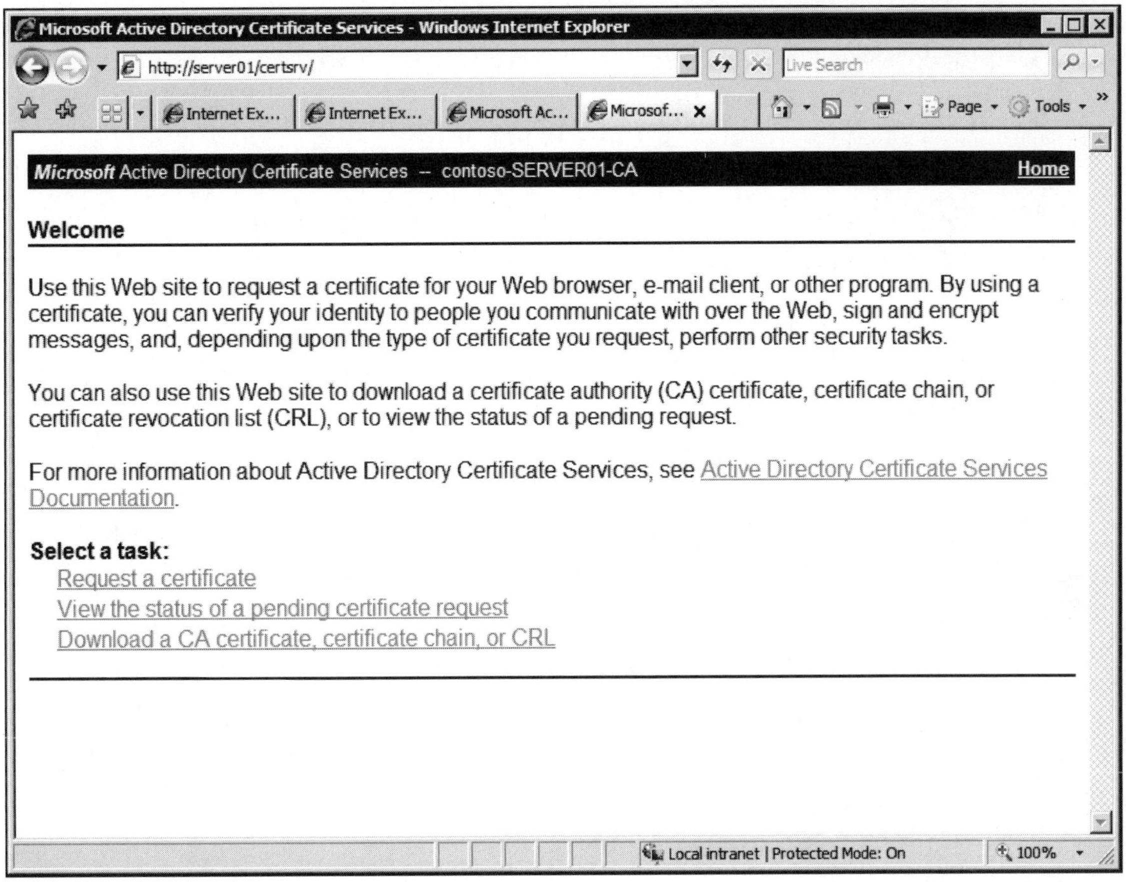

Figure 9-7
Microsoft Active Directory Certificate Services page

3. Click Request a certificate. The *Request a Certificate* page appears.

4. Click Web Browser Certificate. An Internet Explorer Security message box appears, warning you that a Website wants to open Web content using the certificate Enrollment Control on your computer.

5. Select the Do not show me the warning for this program again checkbox, and click Allow. An Information Bar message box appears.

6. Select the Don't show this message again checkbox, and click Close. A Windows Internet Explorer message box appears, warning that HTTPS authentication is required to complete the certificate enrollment.

7. Click OK.

8. On the Internet Explorer toolbar, click Tools > Internet Options. The Internet Options dialog box appears.

9. Click the Security tab.

10. With the Local Intranet zone selected, move the Security level for this zone slider to Low, and click OK. The Internet Options dialog box closes.

11. In the address box, key **http://server##/certsrv** again, and press Enter. The *Microsoft Active Directory Certificate Services* page appears.

12. Click Request a certificate. The *Request a Certificate* page appears.

13. Click Web Browser Certificate. An Internet Explorer message box appears, warning you of the ActiveX control on the Website.

14. Click Yes. The *Web Browser Certificate – Identifying Information* page appears.

15. In the Name text box, key **Mark Lee**.

16. In the E-Mail text box, key **markl@contoso.com**, and click Submit. A Web Access Confirmation message box appears.

17. Click Yes to confirm the certificate request. If an AutoComplete message box appears, click No. The *Certificate Pending* page appears.

18. Press Ctrl+Prt Scr to take a screen shot of the *Certificate Pending* page, and then press Ctrl+V to paste the resulting image into the lab09_worksheet file in the page provided.

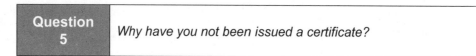

Question 5	Why have you not been issued a certificate?

19. Click the Home hyperlink. The *Microsoft Active Directory Certificate Services* page reappears.

20. Leave the Internet Explorer window open.

21. Leave the computer logged on for the next exercise.

Exercise 9.8	Issuing a Certificate
Overview	In this exercise, you use the Certification Authority console to process the certificate enrollment request you created in Exercise 9.7.
Completion time	5 minutes

1. Click Start, and then click Administrative Tools > Certification Authority. Click Continue in the User Account Control message box, and the Certification Authority console appears.

2.   Expand the contoso-SERVER##-CA node, and select the Pending Requests folder, as shown in Figure 9-8.

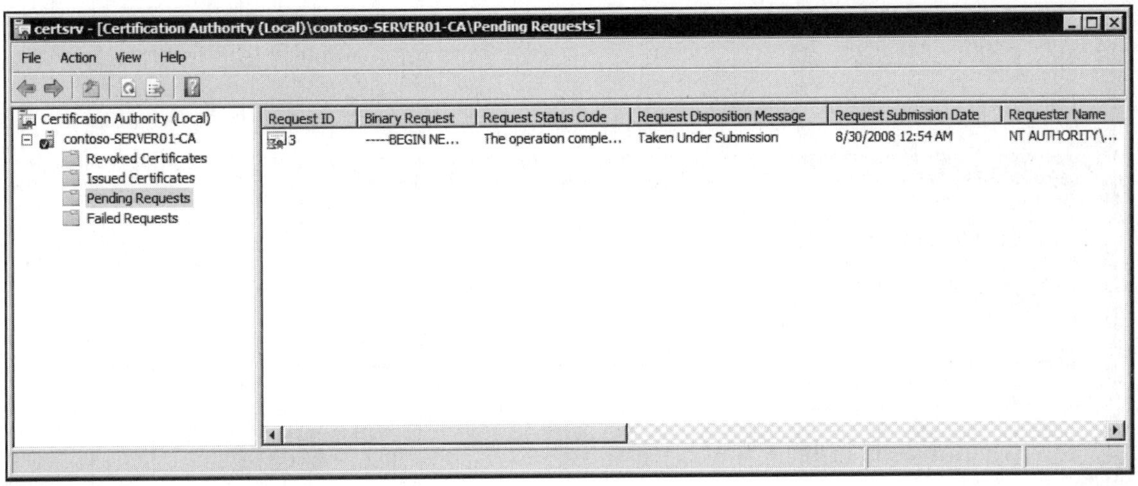

Figure 9-8
Certification Authority console

3.   Right-click the request in the detail pane and, from the context menu, select All Tasks > Issue. The request disappears.

4.   Select the Issued Certificates folder. The request now appears in the list of issued certificates.

5.   Press Ctrl+Prt Scr to take a screen shot of the Certification Authority console, showing the contents of the Issued Certificates folder, and then press Ctrl+V to paste the resulting image into the lab09_worksheet file in the page provided.

6.   Close the Certification Authority console.

7.   Leave the computer logged on for the next exercise.

Exercise 9.9	Retrieving a Certificate
Overview	In this exercise, you use the Certification Authority console to process the certificate enrollment request you created in Exercise 9.7.
Completion time	5 minutes

1. In Internet Explorer, click View the status of a pending certificate request. The *View the Status of a Pending Certificate Request* page appears, as shown in Figure 9-9.

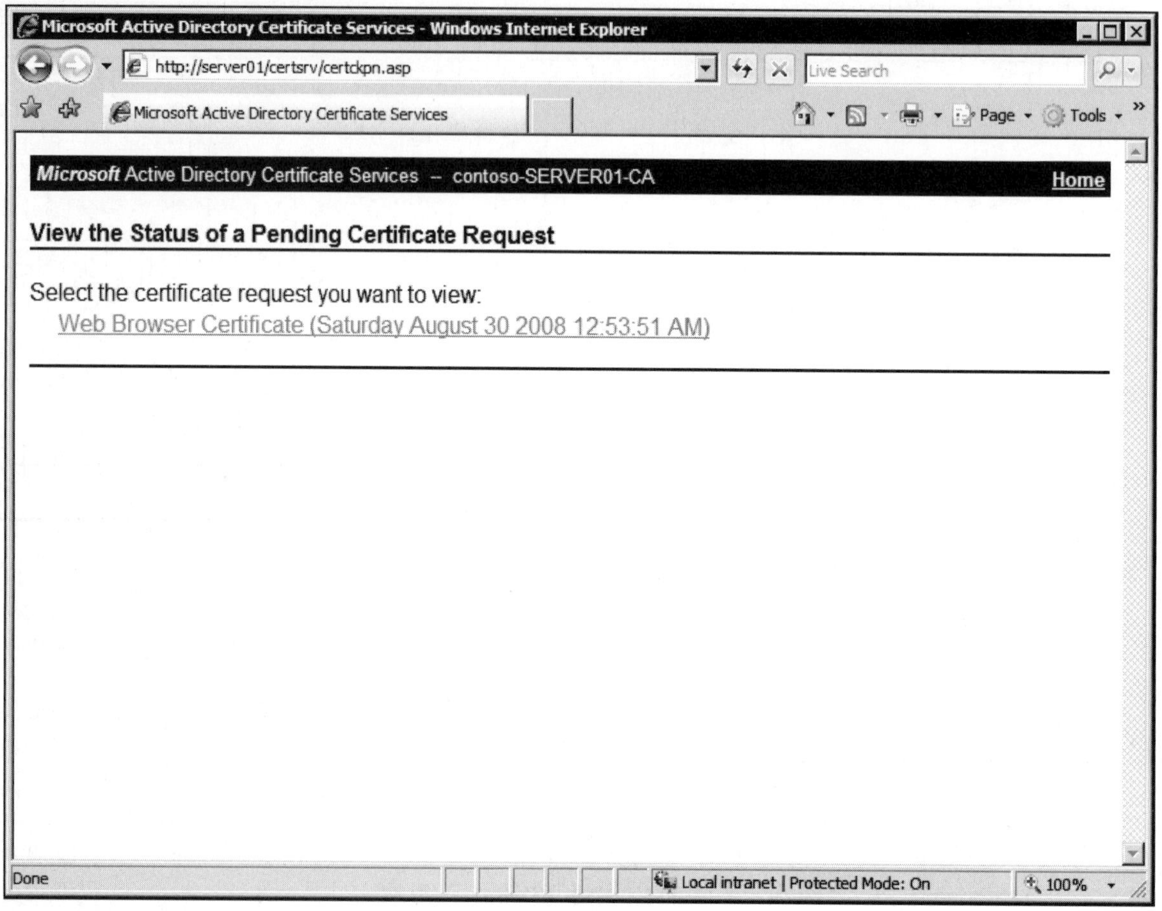

Figure 9-9
View the Status of a Pending Certificate Request page

2. Click the Web Browser Certificate link. An Internet Explorer message box appears, warning you of the ActiveX control on the Website.

3. Click Yes. The *Certificate Issued* page appears.

4. Press Ctrl+Prt Scr to take a screen shot of the *Certificate Issued* page, and then press Ctrl+V to paste the resulting image into the lab09_worksheet file in the page provided.

5. Close all open windows, and log off of the computer.

LAB REVIEW QUESTIONS

Completion time	10 minutes

1. In Exercise 9.4, why was the client initially unable to connect to the VPN server?

2. In Exercise 9.6, why did the certificate enrollment fail?

3. In Exercise 9.6, you looked at a contoso-SERVER##-CA certificate in the Trusted Root Certification Authorities folder of the Certificates console. Why does your CA need this certificate, and what is its function?

LAB CHALLENGE: CONFIGURING REMOTE ACCESS PRIVILEGES

Completion time	20 minutes

In Exercise 9.4, you granted your Student## user account full remote access connection privileges. At the end of the exercise, you reset those privileges by selecting the Control access through NPS Network Policy option. To complete this challenge, you must provide your user account with the privileges needed to establish a connection to the VPN server running on your partner server. You cannot modify the Control access through NPS Network Policy setting. In addition, you must provide VPN server access to all members of the Students group and limit their access to the hours from 9:00 AM to 5:00 PM. List the steps you performed to complete the challenge in detail. By pressing Ctrl+Prt Scr, illustrate the configuration changes you made by taking appropriate screen shots, and then press Ctrl+V to paste the resulting images into the lab09_worksheet file in the page provided.

WORKSTATION RESET: RETURNING TO BASELINE

Completion time	10 minutes

To return the computer to its baseline state, complete the following procedures.

1. Open the Server Manager console, and remove the Active Directory Certificate Services, Network Policy and Access Services, and Web Server (IIS) roles.

2. Restart the server when you are prompted to do so.

3. Open the Server Manager console, and remove the Windows Process Activation Server feature.

4. Restart the server again when you are prompted to do so.

LAB 10
MANAGING SERVERS

This lab contains the following exercises and activities:

BEFORE YOU BEGIN

The classroom network consists of Windows Server 2008 student servers that are all connected to a local area network. There is also a classroom server, named ServerDC, that is connected to the same classroom network. ServerDC is also running Windows Server 2008 and is the domain controller for a domain named contoso.com. Throughout the labs in this manual, you will be working with the same student server on which you will install, configure, maintain, and troubleshoot application roles, features, and services.

Your instructor should have supplied you with the information needed to fill in the following table:

Student computer name (Server##)	
Student account name (Student##)	

To complete the exercises in this lab, you will require access to a second student computer on the classroom network, referred to in the exercises as your *partner server*. Depending on the configuration of your network, use one of the following options as directed by your instructor:

- For a conventional classroom network with one operating system installed on each computer, you must have a lab partner with his or her own computer, performing the same exercises as yourself.

- For a classroom in which each computer uses local virtualization software to install multiple operating systems, you must run two virtual machines representing student computers and perform the exercises separately on each virtual machine.

- For a classroom that uses online virtualization, you will have access to two virtual student servers in your Web browser. You must perform the exercises separately on each virtual machine.

Working with Lab Worksheets

Each lab in this manual requires that you answer questions, shoot screen shots, or perform other activities that you are to document in a worksheet named for the lab, such as lab01_worksheet. Your instructor will supply you with the worksheet files by copying them to the Students\Worksheets share on ServerDC. As you perform the exercises in each lab, open the appropriate worksheet file using WordPad, fill in the required information, and save the file to your computer's Student##\Documents folder. This folder is automatically redirected to the ServerDC computer. Your instructor will examine these worksheet files to assess your performance.

The procedure for opening and saving a worksheet file is as follows:

1. Click Start, and then click Run. The Run dialog box appears.

2. In the Open text box, key **\\ServerDC\Students\Worksheets\lab##_worksheet** (where lab## contains the number of the lab you're completing), and click OK.

3. The worksheet document opens in WordPad.

4. Complete all of the exercises in the worksheet.

5. In WordPad, choose Save As from the File menu. The Save As dialog box appears.

6. In the File Name text box, key **lab##_worksheet_*yourname*** (where lab## contains the number of the lab you're completing and *yourname* is your last name), and click Save.

SCENARIO

Your assignment today in your company's network test lab is to train some entry-level IT technicians in basic server management practices. To do this, you are going to demonstrate how to use tools such as Microsoft Management Console, Remote Desktop, and Windows Server Update Services.

After completing this lab, you will be able to:

■ Create a custom MMC console

■ Use Remote Desktop to connect to another computer

■ Install, configure, and use Windows Server Update Services

Estimated lab time: 110 minutes

Exercise 10.1	Creating an MMC Console
Overview	In this exercise, you create a custom MMC console that will enable the IT staff to access all of the Active Directory domain administration tools in one console.
Completion time	10 minutes

1. Turn on your computer. When the logon screen appears, log on to the domain with your Student## account, where ## is the number assigned by your instructor, using the password *P@ssw0rd*.

2. Click Start, and then click Run. The Run dialog box appears.

3. In the Open text box, key **mmc**, and click OK. Click Continue in the User Account Control message box, and a blank Microsoft Management Console window appears, as shown in Figure 10-1.

4. Click File > Add/Remove Snap-in. The Add or Remove Snap-ins dialog box appears.

5. In the Available Snap-ins list, select Active Directory Domains and Trusts, and click Add.

6. In the Available Snap-ins list, select Active Directory Sites and Services, and click Add.

7. In the Available Snap-ins list, select Active Directory Users and Computers, and click Add.

8. In the Available Snap-ins list, select Group Policy Management, and click Add.

9. Click OK. The snap-ins you selected appear in the console window.

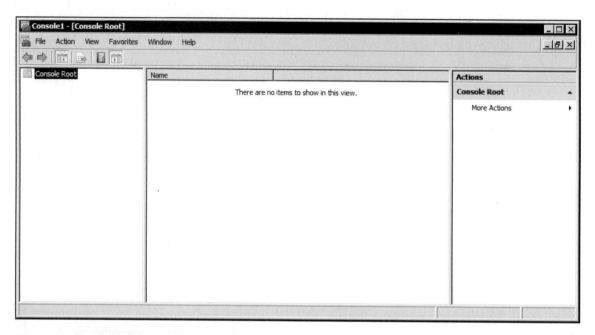

Figure 10-1
Microsoft Management Console window

10. Click File > Options. The Options dialog box appears.

11. In the text box at the top of the dialog box, key **Contoso.com Domain Tools**.

12. In the Console mode drop-down list, select User mode – full access.

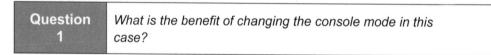

Question 1	*What is the benefit of changing the console mode in this case?*

13. Select the Do not save changes to this console checkbox.

14. Clear the Allow the user to customize views checkbox, and click OK.

15. Expand each of the four snap-ins you added to the console.

16. Press Ctrl+Prt Scr to take a screen shot of the Contoso.com Domain Tools console, and then press Ctrl+V to paste the resulting image into the lab10_worksheet file in the page provided.

17. Click File > Save As. The Save As combo box appears.

18. Save the file to your Student##\Documents folder, using the name **Student##_domain_tools**.

19. Leave the computer logged on for the next exercise.

Exercise 10.2	Using Remote Desktop
Overview	In this exercise, you configure the Remote Desktop capabilities of your server and then use the Remote Desktop Connection client to access your partner server.
Completion time	15 minutes

1. Click Start, and then click Control Panel. The Control Panel window appears.

2. Double-click System. The System control panel appears.

3. Click Remote Settings. Click Continue in the User Account Control message box, and the System Properties sheet appears, as shown in Figure 10-2.

4. Click Select Users. The Remote Desktop Users dialog box appears.

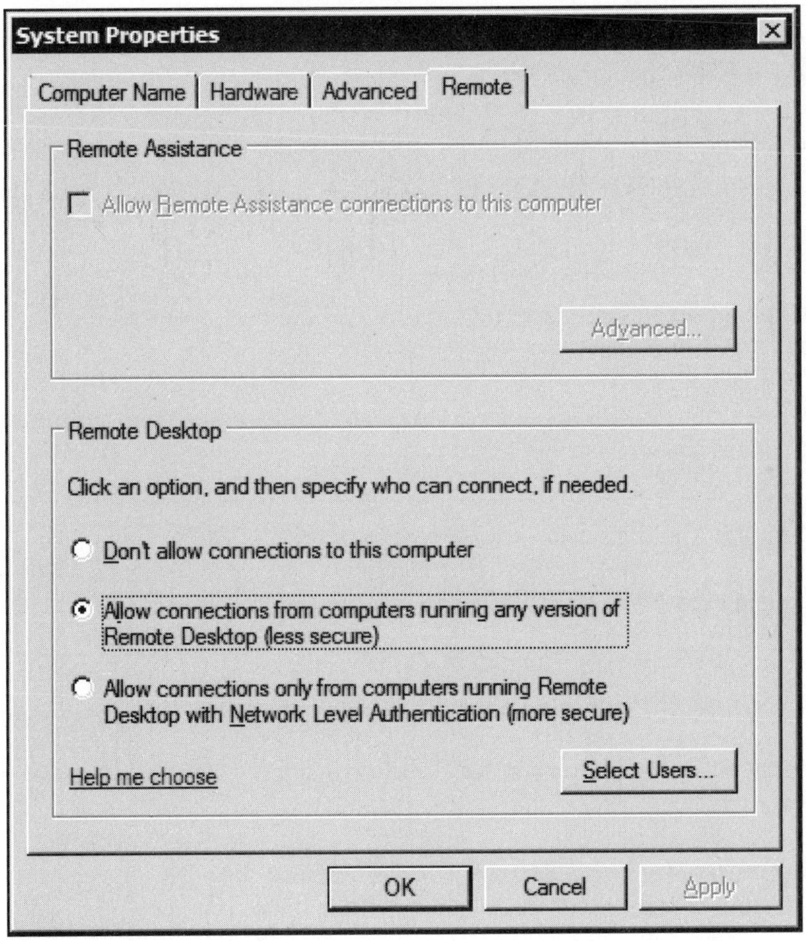

Figure 10-2
System Properties sheet

5. Click Add. The *Select Users or Groups* page appears.

6. In the Enter the object names to select text box, key **Students**, and click OK. The Students group appears in the Remote Desktop Users dialog box.

7. Click OK to close the Remote Desktop Users dialog box.

8. Click OK to close the System Properties sheet.

9. Close the System control panel.

10. Click Start, and then click All Programs > Accessories > Remote Desktop Connection. The Remote Desktop Connection window appears.

11. Click Options. The Remote Desktop Connection window expands.

12. On the General tab in the Computer text box, key **Server##**, where ## is the number assigned to your partner server.

13. Click the Display tab, and set the Remote desktop size slider to a resolution smaller than that of your computer.

14. Click the Local Resources tab, and click the More button. The Local Devices and Resources dialog box appears.

15. Select the Drives checkbox, and click OK.

16. Click the Experience tab, and confirm that the Performance drop-down list is set to LAN (10 Mbps or higher).

17. Click Connect. A Remote Desktop Connection message box appears, asking whether you trust the remote connection.

NOTE	*Your partner server should be logged off before you proceed with the following steps.*

18. Click Connect. A Windows Security dialog box appears.

19. In the User Name text box, key **contoso\student##**, where ## is the number assigned to your computer.

20. In the Password text box, key **P@ssw0rd**, and click OK. A Server## - Remote Desktop window appears containing an image of the remote computer's desktop.

21. In the Server## - Remote Desktop window, minimize the Initial Configuration Tasks window.

22. In the Server## - Remote Desktop window, click Start, and then click Administrative Tools > Terminal Services > Terminal Services Manager.

23. Click Continue in the User Account Control message box, and the Terminal Services Manager console appears.

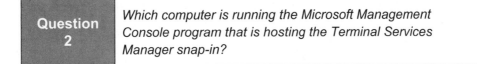

Question 2	Which computer is running the Microsoft Management Console program that is hosting the Terminal Services Manager snap-in?

24. In the detail pane on the Users tab, right-click the Student## session and, from the context menu, select Status. A Status of LogOn ID # dialog box appears.

25. Press Ctrl+Prt Scr to take a screen shot of the Server## - Remote Desktop window, and then press Ctrl+V to paste the resulting image into the Lab10_worksheet file in the page provided.

26. In the Server## - Remote Desktop window, click Close to close the Status of LogOn ID # dialog box.

27. In the Server## - Remote Desktop window, close the Terminal Services Manager window.

28. In the Server## - Remote Desktop window, Click Start. Click the right arrow button, and select Log Off. The Server## - Remote Desktop window closes.

29. Leave the computer logged on for the next exercise.

Exercise 10.3   Installing the Web Server (IIS) Role

Overview	In this exercise, you install the Web Server (IIS) role that Windows Software Update Services (WSUS) requires to provide updates to clients on the network.
Completion time	10 minutes

1. Click Start, and then click Administrative Tools > Server Manager. Click Continue in the User Account Control message box, and the Server Manager console appears.

2. Select the Roles node and, in the detail pane, click Add Roles. The Add Roles Wizard appears.

3. Click Next to bypass the *Before You Begin* page. The *Select Server Roles page* appears.

4. Select the Web Server (IIS) checkbox, and click Next. An Add Roles Wizard message box appears, listing the features that are required to add the Web Server (IIS) role.

5. Click Add Required Features, and then click Next. The *Introduction to Web Server (IIS)* page appears.

6. Click Next to bypass the introductory page. The *Select Role Services* page appears.

7. Select the ASP.NET checkbox. An Add Roles Wizard message box appears, listing the role services and features that are required to add the ASP.NET role service.

8. Click Add Required Role Services.

9. Select the Windows Authentication and IIS 6.0 Management Compatibility checkboxes, and click Next. The *Confirm Installation Selections* page appears.

10. Click Install. The wizard installs the role.

11. Click Close.

12. Close the Server Manager console.

13. Click Start, and then click Internet Explorer. An Internet Explorer window appears.

14. In the address box, key **http://server##**, where ## is the number assigned to your computer, and press Enter.

15. Press Ctrl+Prt Scr to take a screen shot of the Internet Explorer window, and then press Ctrl+V to paste the resulting image into the lab10_worksheet file in the page provided.

16. Close the Internet Explorer window.

17. Leave the computer logged on for the next exercise.

Exercise 10.4	Installing WSUS
Overview	In this exercise, you install the Windows Server Update Services software supplied by your instructor.
Completion time	10 minutes

1. Click Start, and then click Run. The Run dialog box appears.

2. In the Open text box, key **\\serverdc\install\wsus3.0sp1**, and click OK. A Windows Explorer window appears, displaying the contents of the \wsus3.0sp1 folder.

3. Double-click the ReportViewer file. Click Continue in the User Account Control message box, and the Microsoft Report Viewer Redistributable 2008 Setup Wizard appears.

4. Click Next to bypass the Welcome page. The *End-User License Agreement* page appears.

5.   Select the I accept the terms of the License Agreement checkbox, and click Install. The wizard installs the software, and the *Setup Complete* page appears.

6.   Click Finish. The wizard closes.

7.   In the Windows Explorer window, double-click the WSUSSetup_30SP1_x86 file (or WSUSSetup_30SP1_x64, depending on which processor platform your computer is using). Click Continue in the User Account Control message box, and the Windows Server Update Services 3.0 SP1 Setup Wizard appears, as shown in Figure 10-3.

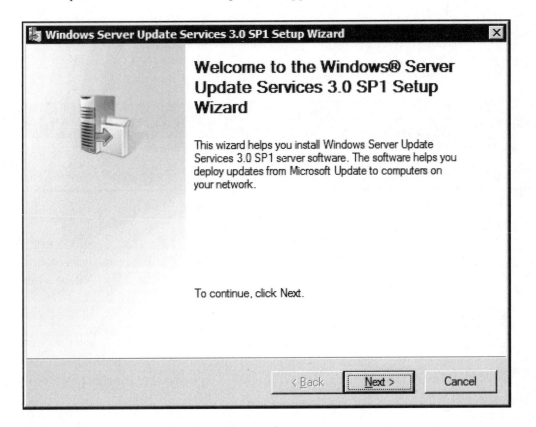

Figure 10-3
Windows Server Update Services 3.0 SP1 Setup Wizard

8.   Click Next to bypass the Welcome page. The *Installation Mode Selection* page appears.

9.   Leave the Full server installation including Administration Console option selected, and click Next. The *License Agreement* page appears.

10. Select *I accept the terms of the License agreement*, and click Next. The *Select Update Source* page appears.

11. Leave the Store updates locally checkbox selected. In the text box, key **C:\Updates**, and click Next. The *Database Options* page appears.

12. Click Next to accept the default settings. The *Web Site Selection* page appears.

13. Leave the Use the existing IIS Default Web site option selected, and click Next. The *Ready to Install Windows Server Update Services 3.0 SP1* page appears.

14. Click Next. The *Installing* page appears.

15. The wizard installs WSUS, and the *Completing the Windows Server Update Services 3.0 SP1 Setup Wizard* page appears.

16. Click Finish. The Windows Server Update Services 3.0 SP1 Setup Wizard closes, and the Windows Server Update Services Configuration Wizard appears.

17. Leave the computer logged on for the next exercise.

Exercise 10.5	Configuring WSUS
Overview	In this exercise, you configure the Windows Server Update Services software supplied by your instructor.
Completion time	10 minutes

1. In the Windows Server Update Services Configuration Wizard, click Next to bypass the *Before You Begin* page. The *Join the Microsoft Update Improvement Program* page appears.

2. Clear the Yes, I would like to join the Microsoft Update Improvement Program checkbox, and click Next. The *Choose Upstream Server* page appears.

3. Select the Synchronize from another Windows Server Update Services server option. In the Server name text box, key **ServerDC**, and click Next. The *Specify Proxy Server* page appears.

4. Click Next to accept the default settings. The *Connect To Upstream Server* page appears.

5. Click Start Connecting. The wizard connects to the Microsoft Update site and downloads a list of available updates.

6. Click Next. The *Choose Languages* page appears.

7. Click Next to accept the default settings. The *Choose Products* page appears.

8. Clear the Office checkbox and the Windows checkbox.

9. Select all of the Windows Server 2008 and Windows Vista checkboxes, as shown in Figure 10-4.

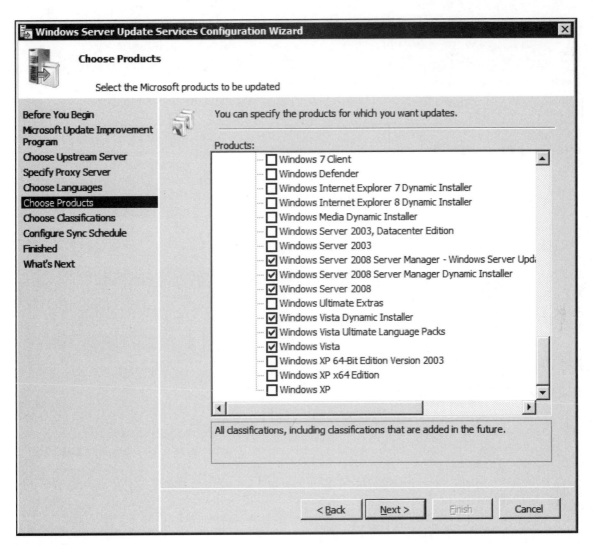

Figure 10-4
Choose Products page of the Windows Server Update Services Configuration Wizard

10. Click Next. The *Choose Classifications* page appears.

11. Click Next to accept the default selections. The *Set Sync Schedule* page appears.

12. Leave the Synchronize manually option selected, and click Next. The *Finished* page appears.

13. Clear the Launch the Windows Server Update Services Administration Console and Begin initial synchronization checkboxes, and click Next. The *What's Next* page appears.

14. Click Finish. The wizard closes.

15. Leave the computer logged on for the next exercise.

Exercise 10.6	Using the WSUS Administrator Console
Overview	In this exercise, you use the WSUS Administrator console to initiate a synchronization event that downloads updates to your server.
Completion time	15 minutes

1. Click Start, and then click Administrative Tools > Microsoft Windows Server Update Services 3.0 SP1. Click Continue in the User Account Control message box, and the Update Services console appears.

2. In the scope (left) pane, select the SERVER## node.

3. In the detail pane, click Synchronize now.

4. Wait for the synchronization process to finish. This could take several minutes depending on the speed of your connection.

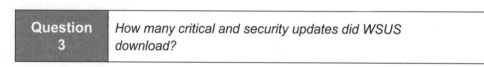

Question 3	*How many critical and security updates did WSUS download?*

5. Press Ctrl+Prt Scr to take a screen shot of the Update Services console, and then press Ctrl+V to paste the resulting image into the lab10_worksheet file in the page provided.

6. In the scope pane, expand the SERVER## and Computers nodes.

7. Right-click All Computers and, from the context menu, select Add Computer Group. The Add Computer Group dialog box appears.

8. In the Name text box, key **Windows Server 2008 Servers**, and click Add. The new group appears under the All Computers node.

NOTE	*Please note that groups you create in the Update Services console are not in any way related to Active Directory groups or the computer's local groups.*

9. In the scope pane, select Options.

10. In the detail pane, select Computers. The Computers dialog box appears.

11. Select Use Group Policy or registry settings on computers, and click OK.

12. In the scope pane, expand the Updates node, and then select All Updates.

13. In the detail pane in the Status drop-down list, select Any. A list of the downloaded updates appears in the detail pane.

14. Click the Classification column head to resort the list.

15. Scroll down in the list of updates, and select the first Windows Server 2008 entry for your processing platform.

16. In the actions pane, click Approve. The Approve Updates dialog box appears.

17. Select the Windows Server 2008 Servers group, and click the down arrow. From the context menu, select Approved for Install, and then click OK. An Approval Progress dialog box appears.

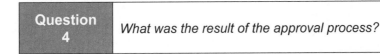

Question 4	What was the result of the approval process?

18. Click Close.

19. Press Ctrl+Prt Scr to take a screen shot of the Update Services console, showing the list of updates, and then press Ctrl+V to paste the resulting image into the lab10_worksheet file in the page provided.

20. Repeat steps 15 to 18 to approve all of the Windows Server 2008 updates that appear in the list.

21. Close the Update Services console.

22. Close all open windows, and log off of the computer.

LAB REVIEW QUESTIONS

Completion time   10 minutes

1. In Exercise 10.2, you used the System Properties sheet to grant the Students group the ability to connect to your server using Remote Desktop. What is another way to do the same thing?

2. In Exercise 10.2, if you selected the Allow connections only from computers running Remote Desktop with Network Level Authentication option, which operating systems would not be able to connect to your server using Remote Desktop?

3. In Exercise 10.5, which settings would you change in the Windows Server Update Services Configuration Wizard if you wanted to configure a WSUS server in a branch office to download updates, configuration settings, and approvals from a WSUS server in the corporate headquarters?

LAB CHALLENGE: CONFIGURING AUTOMATIC UPDATES

Completion time	20 minutes

You have installed and configured Windows Server Update Services on your computer, and you have downloaded and approved all of the available updates for Windows Server 2008. To complete this challenge, you must create a Group Policy object that can configure client computers to join the Windows Server 2008 Servers group you created, access your WSUS server, and automatically download and install all available updates every Monday at 2:00 AM. Create a GPO named WSUS##, where ## is the number assigned to your computer, and configure all of the policies needed to achieve these goals. Press Ctrl+Prt Scr to take a screen shot of each policy you modify, showing the settings you configured, and then press Ctrl+V to paste the resulting image into the lab10_worksheet file in the page provided. Do not link the GPO to any Active Directory object.

WORKSTATION RESET: RETURNING TO BASELINE

Completion time	10 minutes

To return the computer to its baseline state, complete the following procedures.

1. Open the Server Manager console, and remove the Web Server (IIS) role.

2. Restart the server when you are prompted to do so.

3. Open the Server Manager console, and remove the Windows Process Activation Server feature.

4. Restart the server again when you are prompted to do so.

LAB 11
MONITORING SERVERS

This lab contains the following exercises and activities:

Exercise 11.1	Using Event Viewer
Exercise 11.2	Using Performance Monitor
Exercise 11.3	Establishing a Baseline
Exercise 11.4	Viewing Data Collector Set Logs
Exercise 11.5	Using Reliability Monitor
Lab Review	Questions
Lab Challenge	Creating a Performance Counter Alert

BEFORE YOU BEGIN

The classroom network consists of Windows Server 2008 student servers that are all connected to a local area network. There is also a classroom server, named ServerDC, that is connected to the same classroom network. ServerDC is also running Windows Server 2008 and is the domain controller for a domain named contoso.com. Throughout the labs in this manual, you will be working with the same student server on which you will install, configure, maintain, and troubleshoot application roles, features, and services.

Your instructor should have supplied you with the information needed to fill in the following table:

Student computer name (Server##)	
Student account name (Student##)	

To complete the exercises in this lab, you will require access to a second student computer on the classroom network, referred to in the exercises as your *partner server*. Depending on the configuration of your network, use one of the following options as directed by your instructor:

- For a conventional classroom network with one operating system installed on each computer, you must have a lab partner with his or her own computer, performing the same exercises as yourself.

- For a classroom in which each computer uses local virtualization software to install multiple operating systems, you must run two virtual machines representing student computers and perform the exercises separately on each virtual machine.

- For a classroom that uses online virtualization, you will have access to two virtual student servers in your Web browser. You must perform the exercises separately on each virtual machine.

Working with Lab Worksheets

Each lab in this manual requires that you answer questions, shoot screen shots, or perform other activities that you are to document in a worksheet named for the lab, such as lab01_worksheet. Your instructor will supply you with the worksheet files by copying them to the Students\Worksheets share on ServerDC. As you perform the exercises in each lab, open the appropriate worksheet file using WordPad, fill in the required information, and save the file to your computer's Student##\Documents folder. This folder is automatically redirected to the ServerDC computer. Your instructor will examine these worksheet files to assess your performance.

The procedure for opening and saving a worksheet file is as follows:

1. Click Start, and then click Run. The Run dialog box appears.

2. In the Open text box, key **\\ServerDC\Students\Worksheets\lab##_worksheet** (where lab## contains the number of the lab you're completing), and click OK.

3. The worksheet document opens in WordPad.

4. Complete all of the exercises in the worksheet.

5. In WordPad, choose Save As from the File menu. The Save As dialog box appears.

6. In the File Name text box, key **lab##_worksheet_*yourname*** (where lab## contains the number of the lab you're completing and *yourname* is your last name), and click Save.

SCENARIO

Your assignment today in your company's network test lab is to introduce your group of new hires to basic server monitoring procedures. To do this, you are going to demonstrate how to use tools such as the Event Viewer console, the Performance Monitor snap-in, and data collector sets.

After completing this lab, you will be able to:

- Create filters and custom views in the Event Viewer console

- Monitor system performance and reliability using the Reliability and Performance Monitor console

Estimated lab time: 100 minutes

Exercise 11.1	Using Event Viewer
Overview	In this exercise, you demonstrate some methods for isolating the most important events in the Windows Server 2008 logs.
Completion time	10 minutes

1. Turn on your computer. When the logon screen appears, log on to the domain with your Student## account, where ## is the number assigned by your instructor, using the password *P@ssw0rd*.

2. Click Start, and then click Administrative Tools > Event Viewer. Click Continue in the User Account Control message box, and the Event Viewer console appears, as shown in Figure 11-1.

3. Expand the Windows Logs folder, and select the System log. The contents of the log appear in the detail pane.

Question 1	How many events appear in the System log?.

4. In the actions pane, click Filter Current Log. The Filter Current Log dialog box appears.

5. In the Event Level area, select the Critical and Warning checkboxes, and then click OK.

Question 2	How many events appear in the System log now?

6. In the actions pane, click Create Custom View. The Create Custom View dialog box appears.

7. In the Logged drop-down list, select Last 7 days.

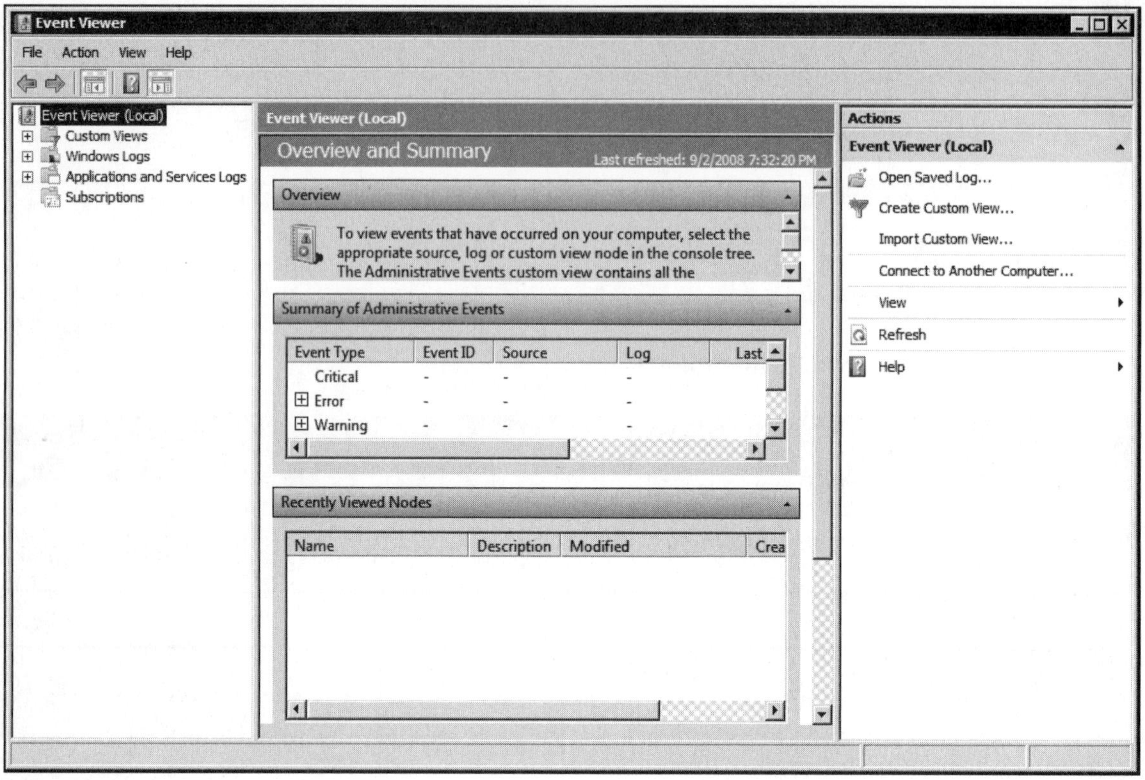

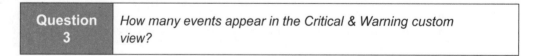

Figure 11-1
Event Viewer console

8. In the Event Level area, select the Critical and Warning checkboxes.

9. Leave the By log option selected and, in the Event logs drop-down list, select the Application, Security, and System checkboxes under Windows Logs.

10. Click OK. The Save Filter to Custom View dialog box appears.

11. In the Name text box, key **Critical & Warning**, and then click OK. The Critical & Warning view appears in the Custom Views folder.

Question 3	How many events appear in the Critical & Warning custom view?

12. Press Ctrl+Prt Scr to take a screen shot of the Event Viewer console, showing the Critical & Warning custom view, and then press Ctrl+V to paste the resulting image into the lab11_worksheet file in the page provided.

13. Close the Event Viewer console.

14. Leave the computer logged on for the next exercise.

Exercise 11.2   Using Performance Monitor

Overview	In this exercise, you demonstrate the company's performance-monitoring policies by configuring a graph in the Performance Monitor snap-in.
Completion time	15 minutes

1. Click Start, and then click Administrative Tools > Reliability and Performance Monitor. Click Continue in the User Account Control message box, and the Reliability and Performance Monitor console appears.

2. Select the Performance Monitor node. The default Performance Monitor graph appears, as shown in Figure 11-2.

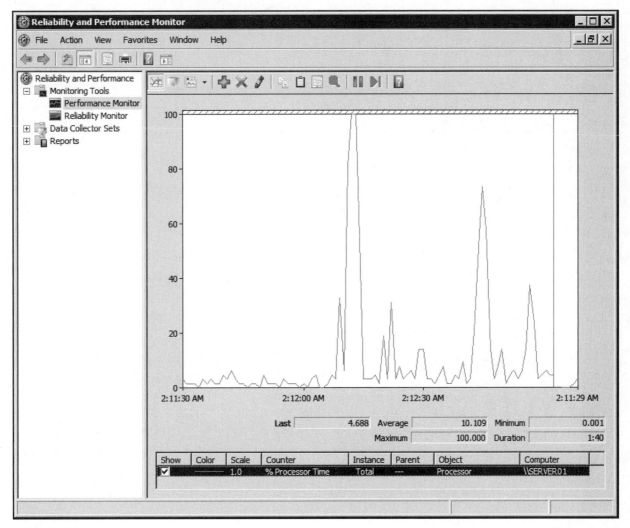

Figure 11-2
Performance Monitor snap-in

Question 4	*What counter appears in the Performance Monitor display by default?*

3. Click the Add button in the toolbar. The Add Counters dialog box appears.

4. In the Available counters list, expand the Server Work Queues entry.

5. Select the Queue Length counter.

6. In the Instances of selected object list, select 0, and then click Add. The Queue Length counter appears in the Added counters list.

NOTE	*Depending on the configuration of your classroom computers, you might or might not see the instances referenced in the Reliability and Performance Monitor exercises. If no instances appear, you can proceed to add the selected performance counters without affecting the outcome of the exercise.*

7. Click OK to close the Add Counters dialog box.

Question 5	*What happens?*

8. Click the Add button in the toolbar once again. The Add Counters dialog box appears.

9. Repeat steps 4 to 6 to select the following additional counters:

   - System: Processor Queue Length
   - Memory: Page Faults/Sec
   - Memory: Pages/Sec
   - Network Interface: Output Queue Length
   - PhysicalDisk (_Total): Current Disk Queue Length

NOTE	*For each of the performance counters listed, the first term (before the colon) is the name of the performance object in which the counter is located. The second term (after the colon) is the name of the counter itself. A value in parentheses appearing after the performance object name (immediately before the colon) is the instance of the counter.*

10. Click OK to close the Add Counters dialog box.

Question 6	*Does this selection of counters make for an effective graph? Why or why not?*

11. Minimize the Reliability and Performance Monitor console, and launch any three new programs from the Start menu.

12. Restore the Reliability and Performance Monitor console.

Question 7	What effect does launching the programs have on the Performance Monitor graph?

13. Click the Properties button on the toolbar. The Performance Monitor Properties sheet appears.

14. Click the Graph tab.

15. In the Vertical Scale box, change the value of the Maximum field to 200, and click OK.

Question 8	Does this modification make the graph easier or more difficult to read? Why or why not?

16. Press Ctrl+Prt Scr to take a screen shot of the Performance Monitor snap-in, showing the line graph, and then press Ctrl+V to paste the resulting image into the lab11_worksheet file in the page provided.

17. Click Window > New Window. A new Reliability and Performance Monitor window appears.

18. Display the Performance Monitor graph in the new window.

19. Click the Add button, and add the following counters to the Performance Monitor graph:

- Network Interface (All Instances): Packets/Sec
- Network Interface (All Instances): Output Queue Length
- Server: Bytes Total/Sec

20. Click OK to close the Add Counters dialog box and add the counters to the graph.

Question 9	Does this selection of counters make for an effective graph? Why or why not?

21. Leave the Reliability and Performance Monitor console open for the next exercise.

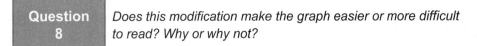

Exercise 11.3   Establishing a Baseline

Overview	In this exercise, you create a data collector set that will capture baseline performance levels for your computer.
Completion time	20 minutes

1. In the Reliability and Performance Monitor console, expand the Data Collector Sets folder.

2. Right-click the User Defined folder and, from the context menu, select New > Data Collector Set. The Create New Data Collector Set Wizard appears, displaying the *How would you like to create this new data collector set?* page, as shown in Figure 11-3.

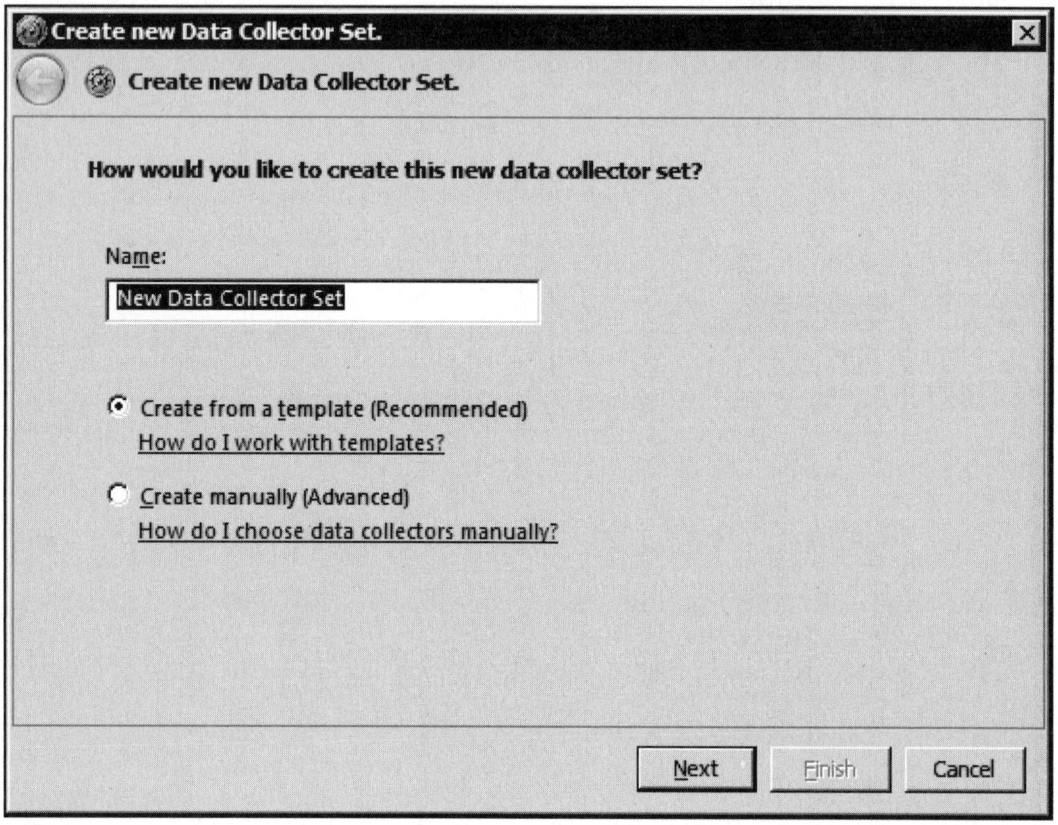

Figure 11-3
Create New Data Collector Set Wizard

3. In the Name text box, key **Server## Baseline**, where ## is the number assigned to your computer.

4. Select the Create manually (Advanced) option, and click Next. The *What type of data do you want to include?* page appears.

5. Select the Performance counter checkbox, and click Next. The *Which performance counters would you like to log?* page appears.

6. Click Add. The same dialog box appears that you used for adding counters in Exercise 11.2.

7. Add the following performance counters:

    *   LogicalDisk (All instances): % Free Space
    *   Memory: Available Mbytes
    *   Memory: Committed Bytes
    *   Memory: Page Faults/Sec
    *   Memory: Pages/Sec
    *   Memory: Pool Non-paged Bytes
    *   Network Interface (All instances): Bytes Total/sec
    *   Network Interface (All instances): Output Queue Length
    *   PhysicalDisk (All instances): % Disk Time
    *   PhysicalDisk (All instances): Avg. Disk Bytes/Transfer
    *   PhysicalDisk (All instances): Current Disk Queue Length
    *   PhysicalDisk (All instances): Disk Bytes/sec
    *   Processor (All instances): % Processor Time
    *   Processor (All instances): Interrupts/sec
    *   Server: Bytes Total/Sec
    *   Server Work Queues (All instances): Queue Length
    *   System: Processor Queue Length

8. Click OK to add the counters to the Performance counters list.

9. Press Ctrl+Prt Scr to take a screen shot of the Create New Data Collector Set Wizard, showing the performance counters you added, and then press Ctrl+V to paste the resulting image into the lab11_worksheet file in the page provided.

10. Set the Sample interval spin box to 5 Seconds, and click Next. The *Where would you like the data to be saved page?* appears.

11. Click Next to accept the default setting. The *Create the data collector set?* page appears.

12. Click Finish to accept the default Save and close option. The new data collector set appears in the User defined folder.

13. Right-click the Server## Baseline data collector set and, from the context menu, select Properties. The Server## Baseline Properties sheet appears.

14. Click the Stop Condition tab.

15. Select the Overall duration checkbox. Then, set the spin box value to 5 Minutes, and click OK.

16. Select the Server## Baseline data collector set, and click the Start button. The data collector set begins running.

17. Select the User Defined folder, and wait five minutes until the status of the Server## Baseline data collector set is Stopped.

18. Leave the Reliability and Performance Monitor console open for the next exercise.

Exercise 11.4	Viewing Data Collector Set Logs
Overview	In this exercise, you demonstrate some methods for isolating the most important events in the Windows Server 2008 logs.
Completion time	10 minutes

1. In the Reliability and Performance Monitor console, select the User Defined folder.

2. Right-click the Server## Baseline data collector set you created in Exercise 11.3 and, from the context menu, select Latest Report. A line graph appears, displaying the data you just collected.

3. In the legend below the graph, select the % Processor Time counter, and press Ctrl-H.

Question 10	What happens?

4. Press Ctrl+Prt Scr to take a screen shot of the Reliability and Performance Monitor console, showing the line graph, and then press Ctrl+V to paste the resulting image into the lab11_worksheet file in the page provided.

5. Press Ctrl-H again.

6. In the legend, click the Object column heading to re-sort the list.

7. In the Show column, clear all of the checkboxes except those of the Memory counters.

8. Click the Properties button on the toolbar. The Performance Monitor Properties sheet appears.

9. Click the Graph tab.

10. In the View drop-down list, select Area.

11. In the Vertical Scale box, change Maximum field to an appropriate value for the data currently displayed in the graph, and click OK.

12. Press Ctrl+Prt Scr to take another screen shot of the Reliability and Performance Monitor console, showing the revised line graph, and then press Ctrl+V paste the resulting image into the lab11_worksheet file in the page provided.

13. Leave the Reliability and Performance Monitor console open for the next exercise.

Exercise 11.5	**Using Reliability Monitor**
Overview	In this exercise, you demonstrate how the Reliability Monitor snap-in evaluates the computer's stability.
Completion time	15 minutes

1. In the Reliability and Performance Monitor console, select the Reliability Monitor node. The System Stability Chart and System Stability Report appear in the detail pane, as shown in Figure 11-4.

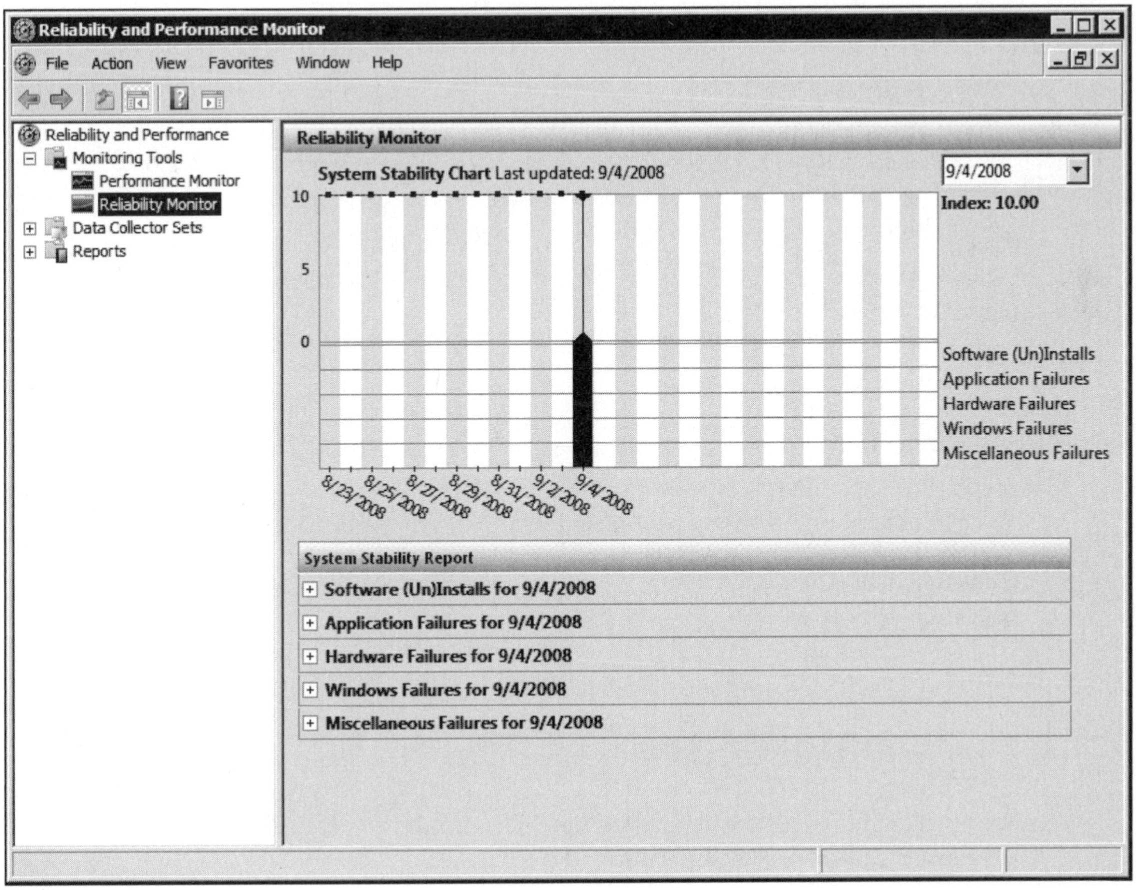

Figure 11-4
Reliability Monitor snap-in

| Question 11 | *What is your computer's current stability index?* |

2. Turn the computer's power switch off without performing a proper system shutdown.

3. Wait 30 seconds, and turn the computer back on.

4. When the Windows Error Recovery menu appears, select Start Windows Normally. Windows loads, and the Shutdown Event Tracker dialog box appears.

5. In the *Why did my computer shut down unexpectedly?* drop-down list, select Power Failure: Environment, and click OK.

6. Click Start, and then click Control Panel. The Control Panel window appears.

7. Double-click Date and Time. The Date and Time dialog box appears.

8. Click Change date and time. Click Continue in the User Account Control message box, and the Date and Time Settings dialog box appears.

9. In the calendar, select tomorrow's date, and click OK.

> **NOTE**
> *Under normal conditions, the Reliability Monitor only processes entire days' worth of events at a time. For the purposes of this exercise, you will be setting the computer's calendar forward temporarily to force the program to process today's events. If you are unable to set the calendar forward, as in some virtual machine scenarios, you might have to wait until tomorrow or your next class to complete this exercise.*

10. Click OK to close the Date and Time dialog box.

11. Click Start, and then click Administrative Tools > Task Scheduler. Click Continue in the User Account Control message box, and the Task Scheduler console appears.

12. In the scope pane, expand the Task Scheduler Library, Microsoft, and Windows folders. Then, select the RAC folder.

13. Click View > Show Hidden Tasks. The RACAgent task appears in the detail pane.

14. Select the RACAgent task and, in the actions pane, click Run.

15. In the detail pane, select the History tab. Then, in the actions pane, click Refresh. Make sure that the task is completed before you continue.

16. Close the Task Scheduler console.

17. Click Start, and then click Administrative Tools > Reliability and Performance Monitor. Click Continue in the User Account Control message box, and the Reliability and Performance Monitor console appears.

18. Select the Reliability Monitor node.

19. Click the red X mark on today's date.

Question 12	*What event appears in the System Stability Report?*

Question 13	*What is your computer's stability index now?*

20. Press Ctrl+Prt Scr to take a screen shot of the Reliability Monitor display, and then press Ctrl+V to paste the resulting image into the lab11_worksheet file in the page provided.

21. Open the Date and Time dialog box again, and reset the computer to the correct date.

22. Close all open windows, and log off of the computer.

LAB REVIEW QUESTIONS

Completion time	10 minutes

1. In Exercise 11.1, how does the filtered view that you created first in the Event Viewer console differ from the Critical & Warning custom view you created?

2. In Exercise 11.2, when you added the Server Work Queues: Queue Length counter to the Performance Monitor graph, you selected the instance 0. Under what conditions would there be three additional instances numbered 1, 2, and 3?

3. In Exercise 11.2, how would using the report view instead of the line graph view affect the compatibility of the performance counters you select?

4. When creating a performance counter collector set, under what circumstances would it be necessary to specify a user name and password in the Run As section of the collector set's Properties sheet?

LAB CHALLENGE: CREATING A PERFORMANCE COUNTER ALERT

Completion time	20 minutes

Your supervisor is concerned that the new workstations in the test lab might not have sufficient memory, and she wants to gather information about memory consumption when the systems are operating at peak capacity. As a result, you have been instructed to log performance data for 60 minutes when the available memory on the computers drops below half of the installed memory capacity. To complete this challenge, you must use the Reliability and Performance Monitor console to create a performance counter alert that monitors the computer's available memory and starts logging when the available memory is low. List the steps you performed to create the alert.

No workstation reset is necessary before beginning the next lab.

LAB 12
BACKING UP

This lab contains the following exercises and activities:

BEFORE YOU BEGIN

The classroom network consists of Windows Server 2008 student servers that are all connected to a local area network. There is also a classroom server, named ServerDC, that is connected to the same classroom network. ServerDC is also running Windows Server 2008 and is the domain controller for a domain named contoso.com. Throughout the labs in this manual, you will be working with the same student server on which you will install, configure, maintain, and troubleshoot application roles, features, and services.

Your instructor should have supplied you with the information needed to fill in the following table:

Student computer name (Server##)	
Student account name (Student##)	

Working with Lab Worksheets

Each lab in this manual requires that you answer questions, shoot screen shots, or perform other activities that you are to document in a worksheet named for the lab, such as lab01_worksheet. Your instructor will supply you with the worksheet files by copying them to the Students\Worksheets share on ServerDC. As you perform the exercises in each lab, open the appropriate worksheet file using WordPad, fill in the required information, and save the file to your computer's Student##\Documents folder. This folder is automatically redirected to the ServerDC computer. Your instructor will examine these worksheet files to assess your performance.

The procedure for opening and saving a worksheet file is as follows:

1. Click Start, and then click Run. The Run dialog box appears.

2. In the Open text box, key **\\ServerDC\Students\Worksheets\lab##_worksheet** (where lab## contains the number of the lab you're completing), and click OK.

3. The worksheet document opens in WordPad.

4. Complete all of the exercises in the worksheet.

5. In WordPad, choose Save As from the File menu. The Save As dialog box appears.

6. In the File Name text box, key **lab##_worksheet_*yourname*** (where lab## contains the number of the lab you're completing and *yourname* is your last name), and click Save.

SCENARIO

Your assignment today in your company's network test lab is to examine the capabilities of the new Windows Server Backup tool included in Windows Server 2008.

After completing this lab, you will be able to:

- Install Windows Server Backup and use it to create full and incremental backup jobs

- Restore files from a backup

- Create a scheduled backup job

Estimated lab time: 90 minutes

Exercise 12.1	Installing Windows Server Backup
Overview	In this exercise, you install the backup software that is included as a feature with Windows Server 2008.
Completion time	5 minutes

1. Turn on your computer. When the logon screen appears, log on to the domain with your Student## account, where ## is the number assigned by your instructor, using the password *P@ssw0rd*.

2. Click Start, and then click Administrative Tools > Server Manager. Click Continue in the User Account Control message box, and the Server Manager console appears.

3. In the scope pane, select the Features node.

4. In the detail pane, click Add Features. The Add Features Wizard appears, displaying the *Select Features* page.

5. Under Windows Server Backup Features, select the Windows Server Backup and Command-line Tools checkboxes, as shown in Figure 12-1. An Add features required for Command-line Tools? dialog box appears.

6. Click Add Required Features, and then click Next. The *Confirm Installation Selections* page appears.

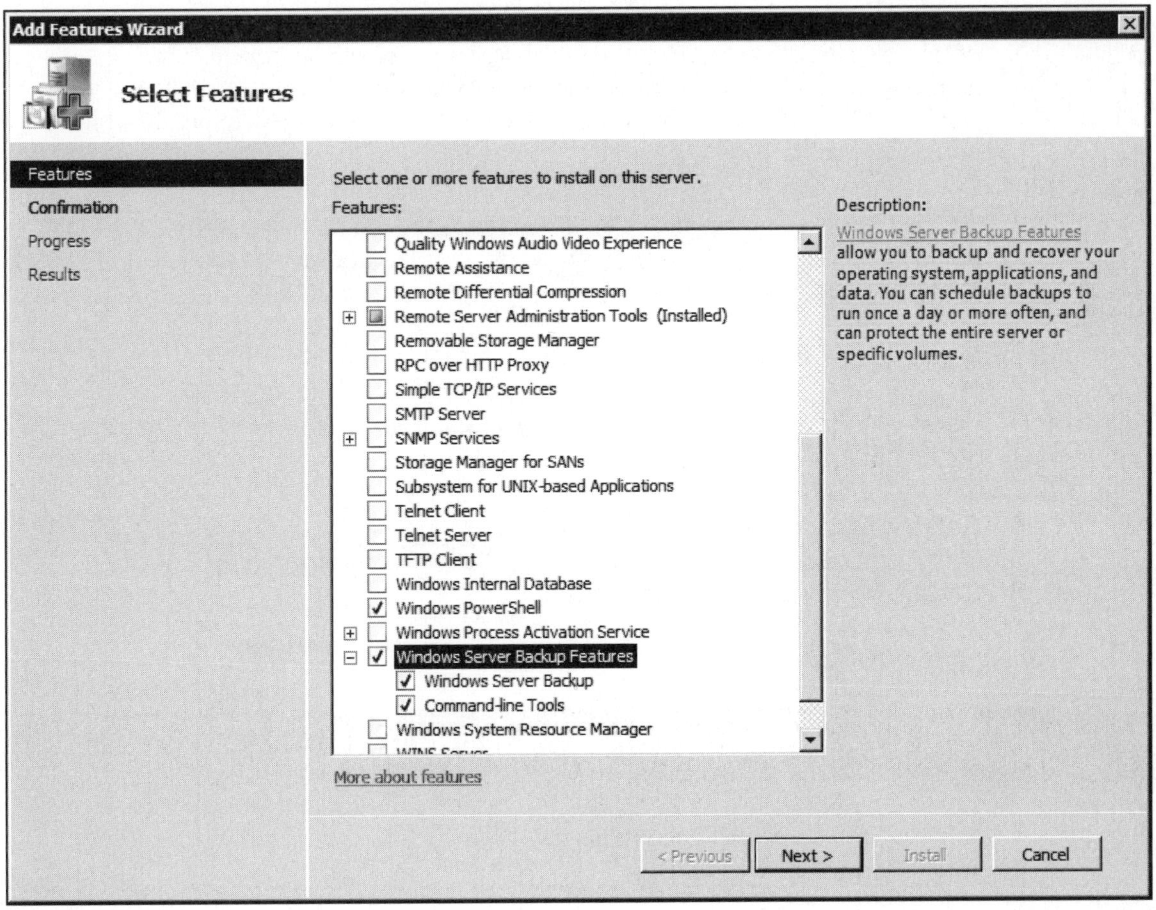

Figure 12-1
Windows Server Backup Features

7. Click Install. The wizard installs the features.

8. Click Close. The wizard closes.

9. Close the Server Manager console.

10. Leave the computer logged on for the next exercise.

Exercise 12.2	Creating a Backup Volume
Overview	In this exercise, you create the volume that you will use to back up your Windows Server 2008 computer.
Completion time	15 minutes

1. Click Start, and then click Administrative Tools > Computer Management. Click Continue in the User Account Control message box, and the Computer Management console appears.

2. Select the Disk Management node, as shown in Figure 12-2.

3. If there are any volumes on Disk 1, right-click each one and, from the context menu, select Delete Volume. A message box appears, warning you that deleting the volume will erase any data on it.

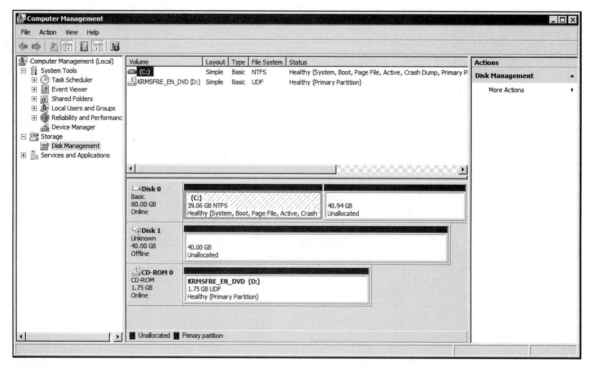

Figure 12-2
Disk Management snap-in

4. Click Yes. The volume is deleted.

5. When all of the space on Disk 1 is unallocated, right-click the unallocated space and, from the context menu, select New Simple Volume. The New Simple Volume Wizard appears.

6. Click Next to bypass the Welcome page. The *Specify Volume Size* page appears.

7. Click Next to use all of the available space for the volume. The *Assign Drive Letter or Path* page appears.

8. In the Assign the following drive letter drop-down list, select letter Z, and then click Next. The *Format Partition* page appears.

9. In the Volume Label text box, key **Backup**.

10. Select the Perform a quick format checkbox, and click Next. The *Completing the New Simple Volume Wizard* page appears.

11. Click Finish. The wizard creates the volume.

12. If there is no second partition on Disk 0, repeat steps 5 to 11 to create a simple volume from all of the unallocated space on the disk, using the drive letter X and the volume name **Data**.

13. Press Ctrl+Prt Scr to take a screen shot of the Computer Management console, showing the volume(s) you just created, and then press Ctrl+V to paste the resulting image into the lab12_worksheet file in the page provided.

14. Close the Computer Management console.

15. Click Start, and then click All Programs > Accessories > Windows Explorer. A Windows Explorer window appears.

16. Right-click the Data (X:) volume and, from the context menu, select Properties. The Data (X:) Properties sheet appears.

17. Click the Security tab, and then click Edit. Click Continue in the User Account Control message box, and the Permissions for Data (X:) dialog box appears.

18. In the Group or user names list, select Everyone. In the Permissions for Everyone list, select Allow Full Control, and click OK.

19. Click OK to close the Data (X:) Properties sheet.

20. Close the Windows Explorer window.

21. Click Start, and then click All Programs > Accessories > WordPad. A WordPad window appears.

22. Enter some text in the WordPad window.

23. Click File > Save As.

24. Save the file to the root of the X: drive, giving it the name **backuptest**.

25. Close the WordPad window.

26. Leave the computer logged on for the next exercise.

Exercise 12.3	Performing a Single Backup
Overview	In this exercise, you perform a single backup of your computer to the backup volume you created in Exercise 12.2.
Completion time	15 minutes

1. Click Start, and then click Administrative Tools > Windows Server Backup. Click Continue in the User Account Control message box, and the Windows Server Backup console appears, as shown in Figure 12-3.

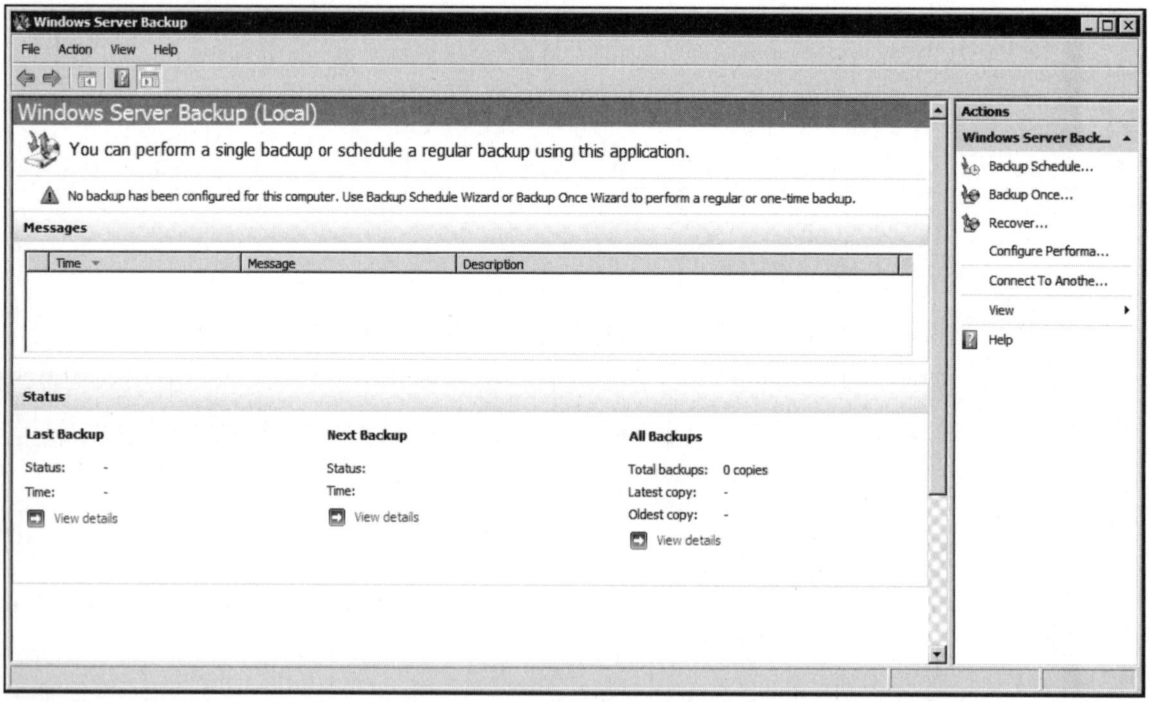

Figure 12-3
Windows Server Backup console

2.   In the actions pane, click Backup Once. The Backup Once Wizard appears, displaying the *Backup options* page.

3.   Leave the Different options option selected, and click Next. The *Select backup configuration* page appears.

4.   Select the Custom option, and click Next. The *Select backup items* page appears.

5.   Select all of the volumes on the computer except the Backup (Z:) volume you created in Exercise 12.2.

6.   Leave the Enable system recovery checkbox selected, and click Next. The *Specify destination type* page appears.

7.   Leave the Local drives option selected, and click Next. The *Select backup destination* page appears.

8.   In the Backup destination drop-down list, select Backup (Z:), and click Next. The *Specify advanced option* page appears.

9.   Click Next to accept the default settings. The *Confirmation* page appears.

10. Click Backup. The *Backup progress* page appears and the backup begins.

11. When the backup is completed, press Ctrl+Prt Scr to take a screen shot of the *Backup progress* page, and then press Ctrl+V to paste the resulting image into the lab12_worksheet file in the page provided.

12. Click Close.

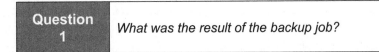

Question 1	What was the result of the backup job?

13. Leave the Windows Server Backup console open for the next exercise.

Exercise 12.4   Running an Incremental Backup

Overview	In this exercise, you perform a single backup of your computer to the backup volume you created in Exercise 12.2.
Completion time	20 minutes

1.   In the Windows Server Backup console, in the Status area under Last Backup, click View details. The Details - Last Backup dialog box appears, as shown in Figure 12-4.

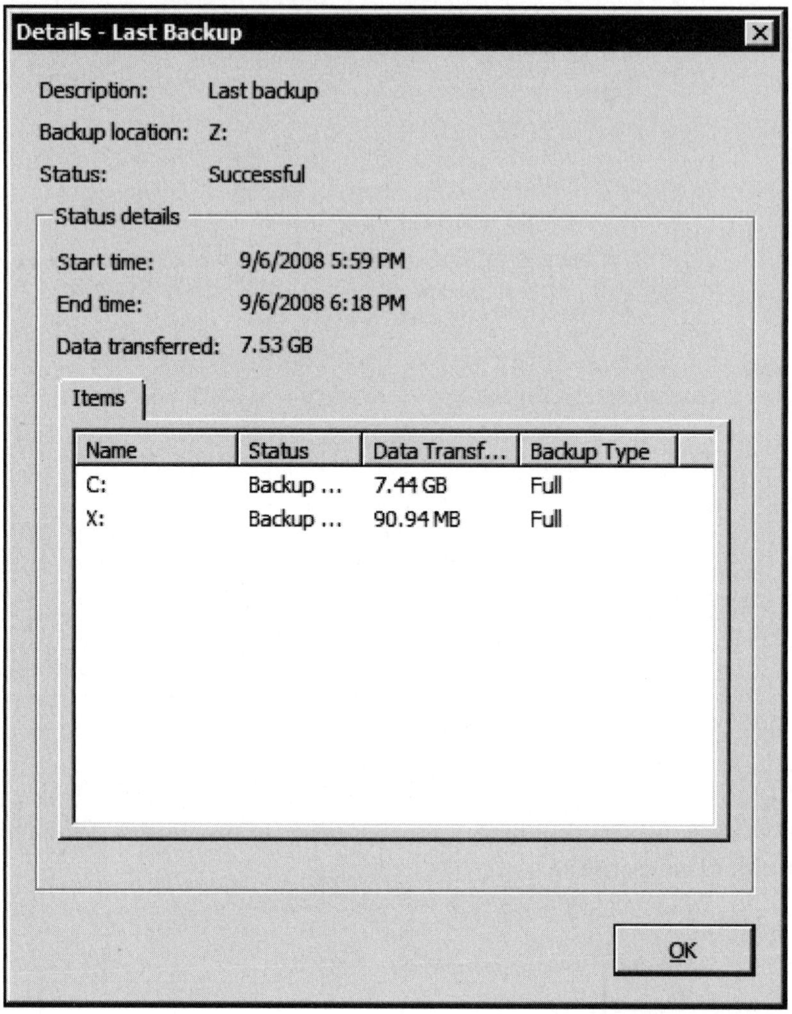

Figure 12-4
Details - Last Backup dialog box

2. In your worksheet, fill out Table 12-1 by using the information from the Details - Last Backup dialog box.

Table 12-1
Exercise 12.3 Backup Details

Drive	Data Transferred	Backup Type
C:		
X:		

3. Click OK to close the Details - Last Backup dialog box.

4. In the actions pane, click Configure Performance Settings. The Optimize Backup Performance dialog box appears, as shown in Figure 12-5.

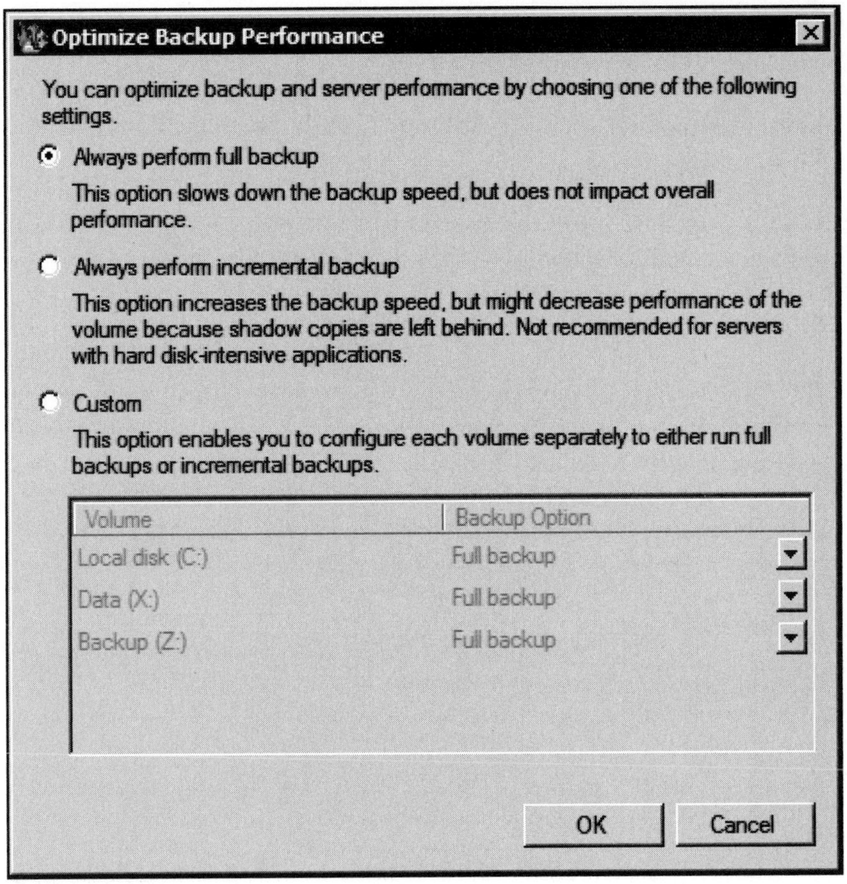

Figure 12-5
Optimize Backup Performance dialog box

5. Select the Always perform incremental backup option, and click OK.

6. Click Start, and then click All Programs > Accessories > Windows Explorer. A Windows Explorer window appears.

7. Browse to the C:\Windows folder, and double-click the WindowsUpdate text document file. A Notepad window appears, containing the contents of the file.

8. Key your name into the top line of the file, and click File > Save As.

9. Save the file to the Users\Student##\Documents folder, where ## is the number assigned to your computer.

10. Browse to the Data (X:) volume, and double-click the backuptest file you created in Exercise 12.2. The file opens in a WordPad window.

11. Modify the text in the file, and click File > Save.

12. Close the WordPad window.

13. Click Start, and then click All Programs > Accessories.

14. Right-click Command Prompt and, from the context menu, select Run as Administrator. Click Continue in the User Account Control message box, and a Command Prompt window appears.

15. In your worksheet, write out a command using the Wbadmin.exe program to execute a backup, using the same parameters you specified graphically in Exercise 12.3.

16. Key your command in the Command Prompt window, and press Enter. The backup begins.

17. When the backup is completed, press Ctrl+Prt Scr to take a screen shot of the Windows Server Backup console, showing the successful results, and then press Ctrl+V to paste the resulting image into the lab12_worksheet file in the page provided.

18. In the Windows Server Backup console, in the Status area under Last Backup, click View details. The Details - Last Backup dialog box appears.

Question 2	Did you just perform a full or an incremental backup from the Command Prompt?

19. Repeat steps 2 to 10 from Exercise 12.3 to run another single backup, using the same parameters.

20. Open the Details - Last Backup dialog box.

21. In your worksheet, fill out Table 12-2 by using the information from the Details - Last Backup dialog box.

Table 12-2
Exercise 12.4 Backup Details

Drive	Data Transferred	Backup Type
C:		
X:		

22. Click OK to close the Details - Last Backup dialog box.

23. Leave the Windows Server Backup console open for the next exercise.

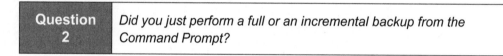

Exercise 12.5 Recovering Data

Overview	In this exercise, you perform a single backup of your computer to the backup volume you created in Exercise 12.2.
Completion time	15 minutes

1. In the Windows Server Backup console in the actions pane, click Recover. The Recovery Wizard appears, displaying the *Getting started* page, as shown in Figure 12-6.

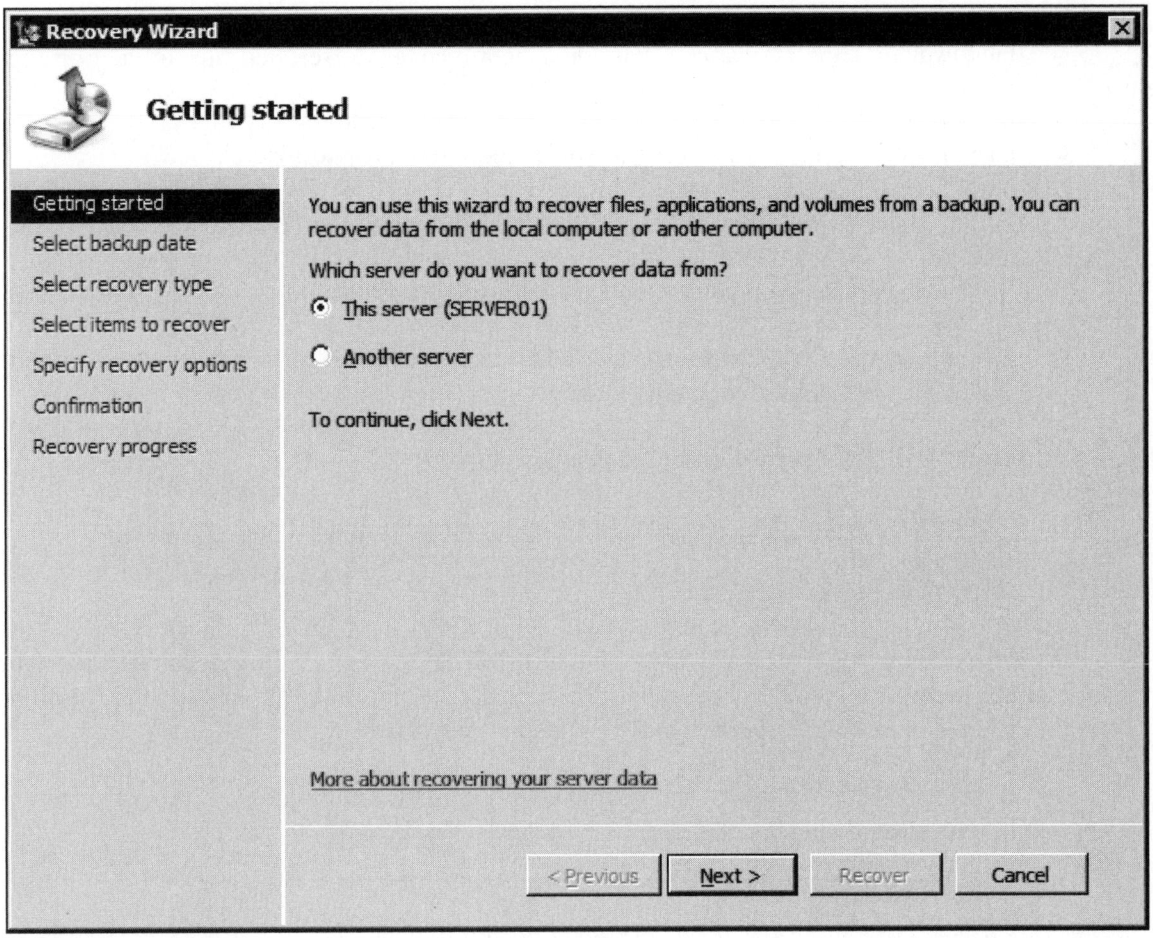

Figure 12-6
Recovery Wizard

2. Click Next to accept the default This server setting. The *Select backup date* page appears.

3. With today's date selected in the calendar, expand the Time drop-down list.

Question 3	How many times appear in the drop-down list? What do they represent?

4. Select the most recent time in the drop-down list, and click Next. The *Select recovery type* page appears.

5. Leave the Files and folders option selected, and click Next. The *Select items to recover* page appears.

6.   In the Available items list, expand the Server## and Local disk (C:) folders, and select the Users folder. The contents of the Users folder appears.

7.   With the contents of the Users folder selected, click Next. A Windows Server Backup message box appears, warning that you cannot recover the selected files to their original locations.

8.   Click OK to continue. The *Specify recovery options* page appears.

9.   In the Recovery destination box, click Browse. The Browse For Folder dialog box appears.

10. Browse to the Data (X:) volume, and click Make New Folder.

11. Give the new folder the name **Recovered Data**, and click OK. The path to the new folder appears in the Another location text box.

12. Click Next. The *Confirmation* page appears.

13. Click Recover. The Recovery progress window appears, and the recovery job starts.

14. When the recovery is complete, click Close.

15. Press Ctrl+Prt Scr to take a screen shot of the Windows Server Backup console, showing the successful result of the recovery job, and then press Ctrl+V to paste the resulting image into the lab12_worksheet file in the page provided.

16. In the console's Messages area, double-click the file recovery job you just performed. A File recovery dialog box appears.

Question 4	*How much data was transferred during the recovery job?*

Question 5	*How can you explain the amount of data that was transferred during the recovery job compared with the amount of data transferred during the incremental backup job from which you are recovering data, as shown in Table 12-2?*

17. Click OK to close the File recovery dialog box.

18. Close the Windows Server Backup console.

19. Log off of the computer.

LAB REVIEW QUESTIONS

Completion time   10 minutes

1.   In Exercise 12.3, why can't you use the Full server option when performing the backup?

2.   In Exercise 12.4, why was it necessary to open the Command Prompt window using the Run As Administrator command?

3.   In Exercise 12.4, why did the Wbadmin.exe program perform a full backup of the C: drive, while in the second job you ran from the console, the C: backup was incremental?

4.   In Exercise 12.5, what would happen if you cleared the Restore security settings checkbox on the *Specify recovery options* page of the Recovery Wizard?

LAB CHALLENGE: SCHEDULING A BACKUP JOB

Completion time   10 minutes

In addition to single, manual backups, Windows Server Backup is also capable of scheduling backups to occur every day or several times a day. To complete this challenge, you must create a scheduled job that backs up your Logical disk (C:) and Data (X:) volumes to the Backup (Z:) volume every two hours. List the steps you used to perform the procedure. After the backup runs, press Ctrl+Prt Scr to take a screen shot of the Windows Server Backup console, showing the job you created, and then press Ctrl+V to paste the resulting image into the lab12_worksheet file in the page provided.